Praise for The First, The Only, '

"*Pam Lilly brilliantly combines her life story with fascinating and powerful illustrations of the pain of racism she has experienced along with so many other people of color. She courageously tackles the impact of racism and offers hope through the power of God's Word. She offers concrete help in achieving hope, harmony, and healing in relationships with people who are different from each other.*"

Dr. Wil Chevalier, President and CEO
LifeBranch Institute International

"*Pam shares her personal story growing up in southwest Louisiana as an African American with Christian parents. Pam opens with prayer, asking for courage and wisdom to tell her story in love and to do so in a spirit of unity. Many of the stories are hard to hear but so impactful. Pam shares without judgment and encourages her readers to ask themselves tough questions. Then, as 'Brothers and Sisters,' let us truly become one in Christ so that they may know we are His followers.*"

Mark Christensen, SPHR
Former Human Resources Manager,
National Diversity Council

"*Pam Lilly pours her heart onto the pages of this powerful work. One part memoir, one part prayer, and one part prophetic word, Pam calls us to break down racial barriers within the church and in whatever communities we find ourselves. By sharing her personal story, we're reminded to remember the first trailblazers who overcame prejudice, and* those who labor as the only and the few, and to follow their lead."

Rasool Berry, Director
Partnership Liaison and Content Developer
Voices from Our Daily Bread Ministries

"In this wonderful book, Pam respectfully and graciously invites her white Christian audience into deeper understanding of a Black woman's experience in America. Through this lens, we see racism is not just the horrific but occasional violent incident reported by the media. She gives us the tools of prayer and scripture to sharpen our discernment to see where and how Christ's Church can and must stand against it in the everyday process of living."

Candace Caley
Christian Business Leader and Bible Teacher

"Pam Lilly is both my friend and my sister in Christ. I urge you to read her story. This is a touching book which will help to move the reader from the shortcomings of our past to the hope that awaits us with our tomorrows. She leads the reader to Calvary's hill where we clearly see that we are each the same at the foot of the cross.

"In these pages Pam sheds a canopy of light on the shadows of heaven that is ours in this present age, calling those in Christ to pray with deepening urgency, 'Your kingdom come, your will be done, on earth as it is in heaven.'"

Dr. Randy R. Butler, Pastor
Mission Increase

The First, the Only, the Few

Why Unity in Christ is Not Always Black and White

Pam Lilly

The First,
the Only,
the Few

Why Unity in Christ is Not
Always Black and White

Pam Lilly

Pam 1967

TABLE OF CONTENTS

Dedicated to My Mom: Rose E. Williams

"Pam, you ought to write a book." Mom's statement caused me to come from around the corner of my kitchen into the family room to see my mother's face. She continued matter-of-factly, "You ought to write a book about the Lord's Prayer." Then without a pause or even a reaction to the amazement on my face, Mom made her case for why I should write a book. At that moment, it was obvious to me for the first time: my mom thought I could write a book.

My mom has always been my biggest cheerleader, from caring for me when I was an infant to correcting me when I was a toddler to encouraging my aspirations and cheering me on to become the first African American cheerleader at Kinder High School. I could go on and on, but you get the picture. So when my mom, without hesitation as she eyed my bookshelf, said, "Pam, you ought to write a book," it took me by surprise. If my mom thought I could write a book, I could, I would, do just that.

The First, the Only, the Few is the third book I've written, with *a prayer journal* being my first book but not yet published. *Mary Morning Martha Day* is the first book I published, and this book is the first book where I tell my story, at least in part. Even with my mom's words ringing in my ears, encouraging me to write the book, I've struggled with the idea of publishing my writings. Who writes a book that you don't intend to publish, one might ask?

Writing is so therapeutic that it is easy to entertain thoughts that perhaps you are writing for your own growth and healing as you process your life experiences and lessons. The battle to write a book, any book, begins with your own thoughts and questions that challenge your audacity to think you can write in the first place, which is quickly followed by the questions, "What makes you an expert on the subject? And who do you think wants to read your book? Or why do you think your story is relevant?" All the while you know you are supposed to write; in fact, not writing is more torture than making yourself sit down, get quiet, and write. Each time I've embarked on writing, I've had to get to this place where out of sheer obedience to God, I began writing, trusting He would give me the words to say and to do so graciously and in love.

Special Thanks

The stories I share in this book happened over the course of several decades and are intended to help brothers and sisters in Christ have conversations that lead to us being united in Christ Jesus. I thank my friends and family who allowed me to use our shared lives, discussions, and interactions to help God's children—the Church—become one in Christ.

To the friends, classmates, and citizens of my beloved hometown, Kinder. I am so thankful that God saw fit for me to be born and raised in Kinder, Louisiana, right alongside you. I had an amazing childhood, and those experiences produced the person I am today. They also prepared me for the world I encountered upon leaving Kinder and living elsewhere. Thank you for letting me use our shared experience to bring understanding and share it with others looking to learn and heal some wounds that have been the source of misunderstanding for so long.

What better story to learn from than that of a group of people from a town called Kinder? Kinder is spelled just like the word *kinder*, but pronounced differently. The adjective "kinder" has two meanings according to freedictionary.com: 1. Having or showing a friendly, generous, sympathetic, or warm-hearted nature, and 2. Agreeable or beneficial.

I realize that as you read the stories within, they may not be how you recall the experience or may even be painful to read. That would be fair as life is not usually experienced the same way even in the same context. I pray that you will understand that in my heart, my intention is to elevate the conversation of unity for the greater good of all people and unity in our country. I offer my childhood story, a story of progression from a time when the citizens of our country lived segregated lives to a time when cultural diversity is common and celebrated. We have come a long way and even lead the way on some fronts. I hope the stories shared here inspire people to keep growing and leading the way to a better future for all.

INTRODUCTION

I never thought our nation would be revisiting race relations in this day and time. And I certainly never imagined being personally involved in a modern-day civil rights movement and race reconciliation. I thought we (our nation) were beyond this deep divide that has plagued this great country for generations.

I feel like I'm being forced to speak into this conversation. I do so with much hesitation. The truth is I have been avoiding and even running from what I believe to be a God-given assignment for several years now. I began to feel like Jonah, a prophet in the Bible who did not want to do what God told him to do, so he headed in the opposite direction of where God told him to go.

I have been running from this assignment because of its sensitive subject matter, which is highly emotional for me. No matter how much I would like to take an incomplete for this assignment, it is not an option. I have finally mustered up the courage to proceed with much caution and emotion and do what I know God has instructed me to do.

The purpose of this book is to tell snippets of my story and give glimpses into my life experience, living as an African American in the freest nation on earth. I am mindful that God ordained the time in history, the ethnicity, the parents I would be born to, and the geographical location of my birth. Understanding this is God's sovereign and providential will for my life, I have always been grateful for the person God made me to be and have embraced who I am joyfully and with gladness, never coveting to be anyone but me—just as God made me.

In writing this book, *The First, the Only, the Few*, it is not my intention to blame anyone for anything, or to accuse anyone of anything, or to cause anyone to feel ashamed, or even offend anyone by anything I say. My intention is to tell portions of my life's story, from my perspective only. I do not intend to presume to know how others think, feel, or even what they understand. I'm simply telling and reflecting on my story as I have seen and experienced it in my life. I hope to carry the theme of love throughout this book and hold every word I write to the standard of love described in 1 Corinthians.

Love is patient, love is kind. It does not envy, it does not boast, it is not proud. It does not dishonor others, it is not self-seeking, it is not easily angered, it keeps no record of wrongs. Love does not delight in evil but rejoices with the truth. It always protects, always trusts, always hopes, always perseveres. Love never fails.

(1 Cor. 13:4–8, NIV)

I trust that God preordained all the days of my life before the beginning of time. And in doing so, God knew the specifics down to the details of where and when I would be born and that my first day in kindergarten would be the first day of desegregation at my school. God knows everything, so He knew what I would need to meet the challenges, limitations, struggles, and ceilings of my day as both an African American and a woman.

He created me with the right personality, attributes, character, persistence, and temperament to handle the challenges life would present. God also knew that my story would be relevant more than fifty years later and that He would ask me to tell it in order to promote healing and unity among His children. Recognizing that I am part of God's reconciliation plan among His children is the only thing that motivates me to write this book. Unbeknownst to me, God has been weaving a relevant story that is my life for such a time as this.

If it were just up to me, I would live an anonymous life tucked away in a sprawling suburb going unnoticed and unrecognized. Yes, I would rather be anonymous. I made up my mind as a young adult not to pursue fame or fortune. I just wanted to live a normal life. But God has commissioned me and even convinced me that He wants to use my life story to bring unity among His children. Jesus' prayer in John 17 inspires me for us to be one in Him as He and the Father are one. I am also motivated by the apostle Paul's plea in Ephesians 2 to Jewish and Gentile believers in Christ to be one in Christ.

It's not that we are against one another; it's just the opposite. We are not for one another, as a family should be. As a child of God and therefore a sister to fellow believers of Jesus Christ, I pray that you receive the words throughout the pages of this book in the spirit I intend them. My words are not meant to cause division of any sort. On the contrary, hopefully they will give insight into the African American experience and not so much for empathy but for greater understanding into an experience you may not otherwise know.

I am aware that words have power, and they can bring life or death, blessings or curses, as James 3:10 states. I aim to choose my words carefully, not to offend or alienate anyone on this journey to unity. Many of the people you will meet in this book are Black, and many are white. However, I have chosen not to label them as 'my white friend' or 'my Black acquaintance' throughout this narrative. This is because I see them as individuals first and foremost and do not want to contribute to the problem I am trying to address

I realize that words may have different meanings and nuances due to cultural differences. Certain words may carry some negative baggage for individuals that I may not know or understand. I will do my best to steer clear of those that I am aware of, knowing it is impracticable for me to avoid all the land mines that hurtful words can set off. I apologize in advance if any of my words or terms trip you up. Please don't let that be a reason to void this message.

Let the words of my mouth and the meditation of my heart be acceptable in Your sight, O LORD, my strength and my Redeemer.

(Ps. 19:14, NKJV)

When faced with an uncomfortable situation described in my story, I pray that you will not just read past it but actually take the time for self-reflection and evaluate if you have ever had such an experience and what role you may have played in the scene. Whether you were the one standing by watching things unfold or playing a direct or an indirect role in a turn of events, we can all search our hearts. And if you are compelled, confess to God and receive His mercy and healing and a renewed mind on the matter, giving way to a more positive path where better outcomes are possible.

Because we are on such a significant journey throughout this book, it's important to accept the invitations to slow down, reflect, and turn our gaze inward, with God as our witness and guide. You are encouraged to delve into any areas of bias or hurt that need addressing. This exercise is not about judgment but about growth. We do this inner work in the presence of God to foster complete honesty with ourselves, free from the need to defend or justify our perspectives. We are seeking a transformation of the heart, a change that can only come from God when we are willing to peer inward and desire to grow into being more like Christ.

My hope is that the experiences I share in this book will open understanding and dialogue so that healing can begin. I hope to set the stage for more conversations, culturally diverse friendships, and cross-cultural relationships that lead us out of the muck and mire that has troubled our country for centuries. Let us begin!

PREFACE

"How do you know for sure this is a God-given assignment?" you may ask. Well, first of all, I would never, on my own, interject myself into the fray of such a volatile and negatively charged discussion. My nature is to be the peacemaker and avoid confrontation at almost any cost. It is not like me to enter into a heated conversation or publicly take sides. A longtime practice of mine is to give people the benefit of the doubt and consider a person's intentions along with their actions.

Second, I heard from God clearly concerning the writing of *The First, the Only, the Few*. In the summer of 2015, I was attending the Institute of Biblical Studies to take some theology courses required by Cru (formerly known as Campus Crusade for Christ), the ministry on which I served full-time and still serve as an affiliate staff member.

My classmates and I arrived at Thursday's class to the horrific news of the Charleston, South Carolina, church shooting the night before at the Mother Emanuel African Methodist Episcopal Church. Because of our limited access to television while staying in the dorms on Colorado State University's (CSU) campus in Fort Collins, this unbelievably sad news was reported to us by our class instructor the following day. We sat in shock with our mouths gaping open and speechless as our instructor reported the news of the senseless killing.

Amazingly, the Bible Studies Methods course instructors were all poised to do a deep dive into Ephesians 2:1–10, but on the heels of this earth-shattering news, they decided to focus on Ephesians 2:11–21 instead. In this passage of Scripture, the apostle Paul deals with his day's race relations issue between Jewish and Gentile Christians.

You can probably imagine the sensitivity of our discussions and the raw emotions that overflowed from our sadness and disbelief of what was being broadcast on television as the story unfolded. The day before this horrific incident, my instructor asked if any of us students would like to have lunch with him because he would like to get to know us better. Being the relational person I am, I signed up for the lunch opportunity, which fell on that same Thursday.

After class I made my way to the cafeteria and carefully filled my plate. Eyes searching for the face of my instructor, I found the table he had selected in a quieter corner of the cafeteria. We said a blessing over our food, and right out of the blocks, my instructor said, "So tell me your story."

How was he to know that those simple words, "So tell me your story," would cause my eyes to sting and well up with hot tears? I began to share from the beginning, and my tears continued throughout the entire lunch, but I pressed on telling my story. I am still unsure why my story, which is an overwhelmingly happy one, invokes such emotion.

This seemingly uncontrollable emotion is another reason for my extended pause and reluctance to write about my life and, therefore, the subject of race. I can't even talk about my story without becoming an emotional wreck. How can you ask me to do this? Just thinking about it causes my eyes to well up with tears and turn bloodshot red. How am I going to get through writing my story if I can't even talk about this without crying?

The day God dropped in my spirit the words *The First, the Only, the Few*, I knew it was to be the title of my next book, and I immediately objected, saying, "No Lord, not another book. And please, not about that." No, not that! Please, Lord, not that! My heart and my head—my head and my heart—screamed out silently. Ache mixed with dread, followed by panic, ran through my emotional and physical being. "Oh no, not that," was all I could silently say as I begged the Lord not to ask that of me. My lament gave way to begging, and begging gave way to reasoning. I sat there, unable to hear the lecturer, unable to fathom how much my life would change. Of course, I imagined the worst—the worst in people, the worst for myself.

"Lord, I can't believe You are asking me to write about that," I said in dismay. I might as well put a target on my back. I might as well run for president. There I sat listening to the lecture on the second pew on the far right side of the church that hosted our classes on our last day. I quickly wrote the title down in my notebook to ensure I didn't forget it or lose it in my lament. I knew in my heart that no amount of begging and pleading was going to change His mind. I had just heard from the Lord, and as much as I didn't want to, I would be writing a book about race no matter how difficult that would be. There was no escaping what I know I heard from the Lord.

My course was being redirected in the most demanding way by words I would have never put together in a sentence. "The first, the only" fired off in my head loud and clear one right after the other like two quick gunshots. "The few" rolled out after a quick second or two to finish the thought. "My life is going to change if I agree to do what I sense God is asking me to do. I don't want my life to change. I don't want to write another book. I haven't even published the first two I've written." The excuses came firing back at God as if to answer the shots just fired at me.

God was not moved—not one inch—by my begging and pleading to release me from this assignment. He would not budge, be moved, or take no for an answer. You see, I had already said yes to God. Yes, whatever He asks of me or wants me to do. I knew in my heart that God had a wonderful plan for my life when I made that commitment to Him, which is the first principle of Bill Bright's *The Four Spiritual Laws* booklet. So I had already committed to God's plan for my life, but talking about race in our culture is such a bitter subject accompanied by an abundance of venom and hatred. People can be so vicious when they talk about race. I don't even want to be a part of the conversation. My tender heart can't take it. I would rather keep my comments to myself and remain mute on the matter. Still, there was no movement on His part. God was silent on the matter. There was no argument from Him. He had spoken!

> *Dear Lord,*
> *Please give me the courage to communicate the things You want me to share as I tell my story in love and do so in the spirit of unity. Allow the message You give me to be received with grace and love. Show us (Your children) Your vision for our relationship with one another because we are all in Christ Jesus.*
>
> *Grant us the ability to focus our attention on the areas we can improve and grow. Help us to honestly search our hearts for beliefs that are not consistent with Your Word. May we look inwardly and reflect on our lives and desire to change the areas of our lives that need renewing.*
>
> *Lord, I want to know Your heart for all people. Please soften my heart toward people I am indifferent to and help*

me care as You do, causing me to respond as You lead me to respond.

I realize this journey will take time and repeated heart checks and adjustments in pursuit of unity with brothers and sisters in Christ. Please help me remain committed to the process so that we may experience true brotherly and sisterly love as Your children. And may our love for all humanity increase day by day. In Jesus' name, I pray. Amen.

The stories of my life that follow have been reconstructed from notes I've taken, dates in years of calendars I've kept, conversations with family and friends, and my own memory. Although I've taken every care to ensure completely factual and historical accuracy, it is possible some unintentional errors related to dates, days of the week, meeting places, and the like, are in these pages. For any that may exist, such mistakes are mine alone.

CHAPTER

1

MY FIRST CRU CONFERENCE

I arrived in Fort Collins on the Colorado State University campus two weeks after completing my courses with the Institute of Biblical Studies for Cru's biennial conference called Cru15. Our leadership courageously embraced an ongoing need to diversify our ranks. This was the year they were going to do something significant to address the matter and begin working toward understanding and solutions.

Sitting in Moby Arena with five to six thousand Cru missionary staff, I was not prepared for what was about to transpire. Cru15 was my first conference with this mission organization, so I was shocked, emotionally overwhelmed, and pleasantly surprised.

For ten days straight the focus and attention were all about understanding ethnic diversity and taking a hard and difficult look at our country and our ministry in light of race relations, and how they impact our thoughts, lives, and work. The fact that Cru was facing this volatile subject head-on from the main stage and even into breakout sessions was courageous on their part but overwhelming for me.

I was so proud, and still am, of Cru for taking such a brave step to be part of the solution, beginning with its own lack of ethnic diversity and addressing the culture that possibly impedes diversity. Conversations on the topic were emotionally exhausting, mentally draining, and heart-wrenching all at the same time for most of us. It felt like all of the attention was focused on me and the few Black staff at Cru. There was no time to prepare and nowhere to hide. We had no warning and no Kleenex to wipe away the emotion that spilled over out of control like a dry creek bed taking on water from a flashflood. Did these majority culture leaders have any idea how emotionally draining this would be for people of color? I do know they had no inkling how those serving from the majority culture would respond. They seemed ill-prepared for the sorrow, shame, confusion, and confessions of white staff members.

As the conference days marched on, everyone began to get a more accurate picture of the reality of the problem that African Americans endured and continue to encounter daily. A teammate asked me point-blank to share my story with my ministry team during our team time. He had no idea what a difficult request he was making of me. At that moment the thought flashed across my mind: maybe the title God had given me was intended to be the title of my talk. "It's not a book title; it's the title of this talk." But my rejoicing was short-lived because I knew in my heart it didn't fit what I heard God say in my spirit.

Nope, I was writing a book, and I might as well begin by sharing my story with my new cohorts at StoryRunners, a ministry of Cru. I knew it would be hard. At this juncture, I hadn't even raised all of the financial support needed for me to report to staff. The only reason I was at the Cru15 conference was that by God's grace I had raised more than 80 percent of the funding I needed, so I was allowed to attend. And just like that, before I officially reported to staff, the Lord added to my assignment.

I approached the small podium in the little meeting room, barely large enough for eight round tables in Lory Student Center. With my story outlined on my iPad and a Kleenex in hand, I approached the podium, laid my iPad on it, grabbed the sides with both hands—one on each side to steady myself—and I began to tell my story.

"I was born in 1963, one hundred years after slavery ended. My first year in kindergarten was the first year of desegregation in my hometown." Blinking away the pool of tears forming in my eyes and fighting back the flood that was ensuing, I developed an urgent case of the sniffles. I knew I would need the tissues. I always do when I tiptoe this close to my feelings. How was I going to do this? Were my tears and emotions making everyone uncomfortable? Or was it my story that stirred the room to tears and the occasional sniffle?

My fellow Cru missionaries felt my pain. They saw who I was and heard snippets of my life. They joined in my story and got a glimpse of my African American experience. They were moved to tears and were visibly affected by my experience and the pain that accompanied it. They couldn't look away; there I stood right before them with my exposed pain and hurt for my new teammates to see.

There was no denying my hurts were real. I was real. They had known me just long enough to get to know me and embrace me. I

17

was the only African American or person of color on StoryRunners' team at the time. As they listened, they entered into my pain. My teammates had probably not considered the road I had traveled and my life along the way that brought me to occupy the same meeting room with them. One might just assume our journeys are similar; after all, we arrived at the same destination. Oh, how the paths that landed each of us there differed.

I would spend the next year or so running from and delaying the commencement of this God-given assignment, and what a time it was. As I, like Jonah, ran from what God was calling me to do, I watched one racial issue and incident after another line up like boxcars on a runaway freight train grabbing the news headlines week after week, leaving me sad and convicted.

"I don't have an ax to grind or a bone to pick with anyone. Why me?" I demanded of the Lord over a couple of years and several chapters into writing this book.

"That's why you," the Lord quietly answered my questioning, as I paced back and forth from my living room to my dining room.

"I have had a pretty good life. I'm not angry with anyone. I'm not upset with anyone," my argument trailed off into a pitiful plea.

"That's why you," softer, quieter tones continued to echo in my head, answering every objection I threw out.

"Lord, You know how I feel about arguing and tension; I avoid it at all cost. Lord, what You are asking me to do will pull me right into the fray."

You will have to pardon me, but I still find myself throwing a tantrum every now and again because it is still hard to muster up the courage to continue, but out of sheer obedience to the Lord, continue I must. I'll bet you this is a *first*, too, to have the author complain and argue his or her way through the entire writing of the book about writing the book. Please forgive me. And thank you for bearing with me along this part of my journey.

Journeys are interesting like that. Many paths lead to the same destination, but not all paths are as pleasant as others. Thank God, not all paths are as painful as others. Recognizing this truth and embracing others' stories can bring healing to our souls and reconciliation to our land.

"To know me is to love me." Roger Ebert

I certainly am not professing to have the answer to this complex, centuries-old issue, but I do feel like getting to really know others is a significant part of the solution. Unlike most books that withhold the solution or prescribed remedy to the problem until much later in the book, I'm going to tell you right up front what I think a large part of the problem is and what I believe will go a long way to begin mending the racial divide that is plaguing our nation today.

I believe we experience division and discord primarily because we do not know one another as individual people. We have not taken the time and energy to essentially get to know someone of a different ethnic background, making it easy to use generalizations like "they always," "all of them," or "those people." Sure, some of us have friends from different ethnicities, but too few to turn this tide of deep division.

The long and short of what I prescribe is to actually make an effort to befriend and get to know someone from a different ethnicity. I'm proposing going beyond recognizing that person and speaking to them in passing. I'm encouraging you to take that person to lunch or coffee and hear their individual story and backstory. Schedule a lunch or coffee break over Zoom. Find out if they have kids and ask to see pictures. Ask where they grew up and what their life was like growing up, and so on. And then just listen to what they are comfortable sharing. Don't try to fix it, make excuses, or even defend your race. Just listen with your heart!

Learn about their culture and ways, and hopefully it will debunk any negative talk you've heard or believe about them and their people. You will be surprised how much you will learn about their people, culture, and history, leaving it more difficult to paint everyone of a particular ethnicity with the same brush. Prayerfully we will begin to see one another as individuals all made in the image of God, each with our own uniqueness but all a part of one race, the human race.

We are all fearfully and wonderfully made by the same Creator for an individual purpose at this specific time in history. Don't you want to know the person you sit next to in the cubicle every day or the family just on the other side of your privacy fence? Don't you want to know the person you pass every day on the walking trail or even sit across from on the bus or train? I can assure you, you will be amazed.

I have just given you what might be the strongest recommendation I will make throughout this entire book. Get to know someone of a different ethnicity and learn all about them. In 1992 Julie Andrews performed a catchy tune in the musical *The King and I*, which was originally composed as a show tune in 1951 by Richard Rodgers and Oscar Hammerstein. The song "Getting to Know You" suggested we should get to know one another with the intent of liking one another. Search for it on YouTube, and I guarantee you, you will not be able to get that tune out of your head, which is precisely what I'd like this thought to do—get stuck in your head and become a way of life for you!

Now that you know a significant part of the solution toward curing our racially sick souls, I'll go first. I'll start by telling you my story around the idea of being one of the first Blacks, one of the only Blacks, or one of the few Blacks, which most accurately describes my life experiences outside of being with family. Most of my life, whether it be my home life, professional life, or spiritual life, has been extremely enjoyable, satisfying, and without regret. However, I have shared a disproportionate amount of my difficulties, not to dwell on them, but to inspire and motivate us to all work towards Christian unity and understanding.

CHAPTER

2

MY BEGINNING

I was an ordinary child born during an extraordinary time in our country. I grew up in a typical place that resembled much of the rural parts of our country, especially in the South.

It took our nation an angry and, at times, bloody century to swallow and begin to embrace the spirit of President Abraham Lincoln's Gettysburg Address. It took our nation one hundred years to go from civil war to desegregation. The idea behind the Emancipation Proclamation only began to take hold after many protests, marches, bus boycotts, and hate-filled words polluted the air. Recall Lincoln's words: "Four score and seven years ago our fathers brought forth on this continent a new nation, conceived in Liberty, and dedicated to the proposition that all men are created equal."

In the small town of Kinder, Louisiana, I was born to Christian parents, James M. and Rose E. Williams. Mom and Dad were some of the first trailblazers into the ranks of the first, the only, or some of the few Blacks to break through color lines in this area of rural Allen Parish. I would be hard-pressed to tell my story without sharing parts of my parents' story. They were also raised in Christian homes and their parents before them. My Christian heritage can be traced back at least four generations. I am the second in the sibling chain of eight. Our home was full of children and full of love. Mom and Dad loved each other, and they loved each of us, but most of all, they loved the Lord. This upbringing made for a happy childhood full of fond memories and great traditions.

Mom and Dad were married for fifty-seven years, and it all began back in Mrs. Eddie Lee Rhodes' Algebra II class when Mom was in the ninth grade and Dad was a senior at Carver High School. Carver High was the all-Black school built in our section of town in 1952. It was the proud home of the Carver Bulldogs. I would have only been a little girl then, but I still remember guys walking the mascot, a real live short-legged, stubby-tailed bulldog, around the neighborhood for exercise. Other days I would bolt out of the house prompted by the lively sounds of brass and drums emanating from the Carver High Marching Band coming up the street practicing their tunes. We lived on the main street through the Nixon Addition community, where all the Blacks lived. This kindergarten through twelfth-grade school, Carver provided many jobs for families, including my paternal grandmother, who worked in the cafeteria preparing delicious food for the students. Eola Peters was a great cook.

The late Mrs. Eddie Lee Rhodes was fond of both my mom and my dad. Dad said, "I was a sickly kid, and so I missed school a lot," and for that reason he found himself in the Algebra II class with the beautiful and smart Rose Ella Johnson. This would set Dad up to meet and get to know the girl of his dreams and the love of his life. Realizing that Dad liked her, Mom said, "Mrs. Rhodes paired us up by sitting your dad right behind me, and she told me, 'You better make sure he gets through my class.'"

Then one day Dad bought Mom a Coca-Cola, and she accepted it. It was a big deal for a young man to buy a girl a Coke in those days. Dad went on to buy Mom a Coke every day from then on. Once he graduated, Dad made sure Mom had Coke money every day. He didn't want anyone else to buy her a Coke.

Mom's parents divorced when she was a young girl, and she and her siblings stayed with her father in Kinder. The good-looking Willie Johnson worked for the Southern Pacific Railroad and made good money for a Black man back in those days. During her junior year in high school Mom went to live with her mother, Irene, who had fought and won her battle with tuberculosis. She was not expected to live or ever return from hospital quarantine in Lafayette. But months later she beat the disease and returned to her home in Lake Charles, about a thirty-minute drive from Kinder.

Dad continued to supply Mom with Coke money for the week when he saw her on the weekends. He wanted to be the only one who provided for her. Having her own money gave Mom independence and confidence that would follow her throughout her life. These are the parents who raised me, the dependable provider James Williams and the confidently independent Rose Williams.

Attending W. O. Boston High School after the move proved to be a pivotal point in Mom's life because that's where she learned how to type. Being a quick study, she picked up typing right away. Learning this skill set her apart a decade later when the affirmative action policy forced schools accepting Title I funding to hire a certain number of Blacks in specific positions. Mom's ability to type, and type well, qualified her for a Title I teacher's aide position at Kinder High School in the mid-1970s, as one of only two Black teachers aides the school hired.

Mom went on to become the first Black to work at her bank and worked her way up through the ranks to eventually become the first Black branch manager at this particular bank. Mom was always amazing to me. Her skills included sewing, cooking, baking, preserving fruits and vegetables, making confectionaries, decorating, and many more. She always seemed to have it all together. She could do whatever she set her mind to and did it with ease. Mom exuded confidence with a smile. Her house was always immaculate, and she could make a little go a long way. Budgeting for such a large family was no easy task, but she did it and always seemed to have extras to be generous.

Similarly, Dad was an extremely hard worker and learned just as quickly, picking up one skill after another. He would spend thirty-plus years working himself up to crew foreman at Tennessee Gas Pipeline, which later became El Paso Gas, and is now a Kinder Morgan company. Dad was not only great with his hands but was also quite the outdoorsman. He was the ultimate fisherman, hunter, gatherer, and gardener, which provided a variety for our dinner table. And to top it all off, Dad was and is an excellent cook. You can ask anyone around town about his gumbo, rice dressing (dirty rice), and sauce piquante, just to name a few.

As a young child and on into my young teen years, I watched Mom and Dad work together as an incredible tag team to accomplish and provide for our family. They provided a wholesome Christian home for my siblings and me to grow up with plenty of affirmation and love. The church was only a few doors down the street, and every time those doors were open, we were there for church, choir rehearsal, Bible school, Sunday school, Baptist Training Union, and Vacation Bible School. You name it, we were there. It was easy to be a kid and learn about God in my community. Generations of loving grandparents, aunts, uncles, and cousins were all around on every side. Weekends and holidays were filled with family and food galore. Collectively, this life made for a loving and stable environment.

While a couple hundred thousand people made their way to the March on Washington, I was just days from being born. Unbeknownst to me, an infant crying out for nourishment, a people—my people—cried out in the streets for equality. Mom and Dad must have censored what we heard as toddlers, or I was just too young to remember because I was unaware that such strife was happening and threatening to spill over into our lives at any moment.

But that was then, and this is now sixty years later. Who would have thought that on the heels of the first African American president, Barack Obama, we would begin experiencing a firestorm of cultural divide in our country? Who would have thought we would be revisiting race relations in our country in every subsequent year since then?

As my story spills out, thoughts flooded with happy memories overwhelm me to the point of tender tears of gratitude. My childhood was graced with two parents in a home full of joy, great food, present grandparents, plenty of siblings and cousins, beautiful traditions, and words of affection. My creative mother and resourceful father were all-loving and affectionate. We were going places and experiencing things, as much as was allowed back then. Lots of encouragement, teaching, and wisdom were passed down to me from people who wanted the best for me.

Life is good, it is consistently very good, but like the stain of Communion wine on a white Easter dress, the stain of prejudice faintly taints my life story.

Hopefully, spilling my heart out will matter, and lives will be changed. Under God's watchful eye, I pilfer through the backstory of my life and unpack my experiences and my hurt feelings that I had so neatly folded and put away in the invisible drawers of my mind. Prayerfully, the telling of my story will be used to teach us a few things about ourselves. I have not thought about most of what I share since it happened, save for the occasional déjà vu moment, or as God has called it to my attention while writing this book.

Naturally, I hope I will be more fully known and understood. But, more importantly, I hope you don't miss out on the part of God's grand imagination that created me and people who look like me—that part of God that has the capacity to create and to love me. Please don't dislike or dismiss someone our Lord loves. Thankfully, He is full of grace and forgiveness; that is who He is. I choose to focus on who He is and to be obedient to His call on my life. He is God!

CHAPTER

3

MY FIRST DAY OF SCHOOL

We were all excited and scared, happy and sad. Black and white kids alike were excited and happy because it was our first day of school, but we were scared, sad, and even clingy to our mommies when it was time for them to leave. White and Black kids responded the same way on their first day of school to being left with their teachers in what seemed to kindergarteners like a supersized cafeteria. Unbeknownst to us, with tears streaming down our faces, we were breaking new ground and blazing a new trail in our town and country. Our desegregated lives would forever be what we, the future class of 1981, would know as normal.

Mom and Dad had the option to send me to kindergarten at Carver Elementary in our neighborhood within the confines of one quadrant of town known as the quarters, defined by the train tracks that crisscrossed the town. But instead, Mom sent me to Kinder Elementary School just across the railroad tracks. It was an optional year for Blacks to attend the white school to continue the transition of desegregating the white school. Mom insisted that my older sister, who was in the first grade, and I attend the white school immediately. Having never attended an all-Black school forced me to begin the assimilation process into the majority culture at the young and tender age of five. Of course, at five, I didn't see it as assimilating into the majority culture; I was just a shy kid experiencing my first day of school like every other kid my age.

This same day was proving to be anything but ordinary for others who had only attended all-Black or all-white schools. Most people my age and older can remember the first day of school desegregated in their town or city. If you can't remember it, I'm sure you have seen footage of the first day(s) of school desegregation on television or on the internet that has left the image stamped in your memory. Black students were met with resistance at the higher grade levels. Violence forever colored the era in which schools were desegregated across the country, and especially in the South.

Unlike the story that played out in the news, my first day of school was graced by the beautiful, kind, and soft-spoken Mrs. Kay Sonnier. It also helped to have Mrs. Wakely just down the hall teaching her first-grade class. My mom used to clean Mrs. Wakely's house, and my sister and I knew all the Wakely children. My mom and Mrs. Wakely loved each other, and they loved each other's kids. She was sweet but stern. Just knowing she was there and getting glimpses of her in the hall and lunchroom throughout the day was reassuring.

It's hard for me to believe that it was not until well into my adult life that I fully comprehended the historical significance of that particular day. I guess that's because I can instantly recall it with fond memories what was such a vivid first day of school for me. Yet I know others experienced a different reality, and many have physical and emotional scars as hateful reminders. We were not all having the same experience. It was the same day, same town, but a different experience. We've all had a *first day of school* experience, and some of us had a *first day of school desegregation* experience that we can recall at will.

Take some time and recall that day and what it was like for you. Then think about what it may have been like for others, and especially minorities. What adjectives would you use to describe your day, and what adjectives would you use to describe the minorities' experience that day? Are you able to envision how afraid and alone they may have felt? Or how much courage, bravery, and guts it would have taken to enter a place where it was vehemently evident that you were not wanted?

Recalling this painful history is not an exercise in shame or guilt but in connecting with our past. Here is a chance to reflect on what transpired that day and recognize who we were and what roles we played on such a day, even if that sentiment was indifference or, like me, you were unaware of its full magnitude until much later in life. Let's look inside and deal with how thinking about this day makes us feel now and how others may have felt about that day, realizing it was the same day, but not everyone was having the same experience. What individuals from my generation experienced that day was probably vastly different. We can only revisit our particular reality, but we can imagine how others may have experienced that day.

CHAPTER

4

FIRST IN CHARGE

"**N**ow, James, you are going to have to keep a low profile because these guys are not used to a Black man working in their department," the superintendent instructed my dad on his first day of work. "So, I just played along with it," Dad said, "and went along with them, and they got to likin' me and stuff like that, you know." Dad was the first Black man Tennessee Gas Pipeline hired to work in the crew at that location, just outside of Kinder and outside the Allen Parish line.

"Before that, I was working as a concrete finisher building bridges in Calcasieu Parish near Moss Bluff with T. Miller. And for a little while, before I started working at Tennessee Gas, I worked way up past Baton Rouge and Scotlandville, almost to Saint Francisville. Me and some other guys used to get up at 4:00 in the morning every day and make that drive." Turning toward me, he said, "Remember, I had that red-looking Wildcat." I nodded my head in agreement, searching my memory for the only old red car I can remember. I was just a little girl back then.

"That was right after the Martin Luther King Jr. thing," in 1968, he said. They couldn't discriminate anymore, and they had to hire one Black. I noticed he didn't say after Martin Luther King Jr. was killed. Perhaps he was subconsciously unable to say it without getting bogged down in the emotions of it all. When I think about the struggles of raising a young family, trying to put food on the table, all the while being suppressed by the system you are born into, the pride in my dad swells up in me and results in tears welling up in my eyes. You and I can only imagine what this young, skinny, twenty-something, dark-skinned guy must have endured on and off the job. But he never quit, and I don't ever remember hearing him complain.

"These boys ain't never worked with no Black person in their department, and they don't work with them period, out here," the superintendent said to Uncle Lucious. "So, if you don't bring me somebody good out here, I'm going to swell your head."

"That was just a joke, though," Dad said. My uncle was already working there as the janitor, and he was charged with finding just the right person who would get along well with the all-white crew.

"Me and Uncle Lucious were best friends, and of course, Aunt Ida and your mom was kin. They were not supposed to hire kinfolks, but I was just an in-law, so he chose me. Now that caused some problems with one of our other friends because he [Uncle Lucious] chose me. That really broke their friendship up, and it never did get back to the way it was," Dad sadly recounts.

My great-uncle by marriage, Uncle Lucious had gone into military service and had come back home. "They had to hold his job for him," Dad explained. He had been there a total of seventeen years, and when he came back from the service, the superintendent told him, "We can't work you as a janitor anymore," so he went into operations, and my dad started in the compressor department. The year was 1969.

I often wonder what it must have been like for Dad in 1969. I was only five years old, not quite six. As I was in kindergarten at the newly desegregated school, Dad was navigating the treacherous waters of uncertainty at his new job. We both had a job to do, me at school and him at work. That job was to get along with the white folks, those in charge and those alongside us, those who despised us and those who just tolerated us, and those who didn't mind making a place for us.

Years later, Dad said optimistically, "That first day was a pretty good day. But there wasn't a whole lot of talking going on, especially between some of the people that were known to be prejudiced against Blacks. Some of them didn't like it that much. Some of them never got used to a Black man in the crew with them, but most of them—90 percent of them—did get used to it."

Dad told me, "I knew a lot of them white boys because I worked cleaning offices and stores around town since I was thirteen. I cleaned the drug store, the post office, the insurance office, and the hardware store after school, and they were used to me being around. So, when I started working at Tennessee Gas, a lot of them accepted me because they knew me already."

With fondness, he told me, "We had thirteen big engines pumping natural gas all over the world." In his last fifteen or so years, he was "in charge of the crew," as he would call it. "Some of them guys way back then…didn't care about working for Black folks. They were hard on me and my own people were hard on me too; they didn't like taking orders from a Black man. You had to break down barriers, you know." Dad was a master at breaking down those barriers that divide, and his relationships with his co-workers and friends continue until today. Oh, how times have changed for the better for Black folks over the years. Dad would retire some thirty-five years later when Tenneco Gas Pipeline sold to El Paso Gas. He was the senior technician in his division. He continued working as a contractor and consultant for El Paso Gas to put my younger siblings through college.

"You were the only one of my children that didn't get to go to college," Dad sometimes said as if regretful. But I have no regrets. He gave me what he had, a strong work ethic and a keen ability to get along with white folks. And at the time it was the most valuable education I needed. Opportunities were just beginning to open up for Blacks; and education or no education, only those who knew how to fit in made it in these all-white spaces.

My dad and mom made sure we knew how to navigate, survive, and even thrive in school and on the job. It was not only about the ability to get the job, but you had to know how to keep the job. And back then, that took knowing your place and not overstepping the boundaries that were being newly drawn. Just because the color lines were finally being redrawn more favorably on paper to include Blacks did not necessarily mean white people's hearts had changed toward us. We still had a way to go as far as that was concerned. The truth be told, we still have a way to go even now.

Mom and Dad were some of the first Blacks who represented our people in their workplaces. Our entire race was being judged by the performance of a few Black people's abilities to get along and survive in the newly desegregated America. There was tension on every side. Companies were made to hire you and give you a chance to prove yourself. On the other hand, that chance was usually only afforded to one Black. What about the rest? Did they not deserve a chance too?

Imagine the bitterness that settles in, one against another, when systematically, according to the mandate, only one is chosen from among your people. Imagine the hopelessness that becomes a reality when the *one Black* quotas are met, and you are still stuck in a menial job that pays next to nothing.

I take a break from my writing to clear my head from the deep pit into which I had just plummeted. I fix myself a serving of Greek vanilla yogurt with granola sprinkled in and return to my computer to find my screen saver displaying a beautiful picture of the Paris skyline showing off the grandeur of the Eiffel Tower. Taking it all in, I am reminded of my trips to Paris and a slew of other world-renowned destinations I have enjoyed in my travels. I am reminded that we have come "a mighty long way," as my ancestors would say. But the luxury of that reality has only been afforded to a few within my race. Truthfully, this statement is probably also true among the haves and have-nots within white America and other ethnicities as well.

This American dream is not afforded to all peoples equally. To think it ever could be is naïveté. Naive or not, when it is not offered to you, it could feel like you are playing the part of an extra in someone else's dream. We live in the same country, attend the same schools, drive on the same streets, and work side-by-side in cubicles or on assembly lines, but we are simply not all having the same experience.

CHAPTER

5

MY FIRST OCCUPATION

"The first thing you ever said you wanted to be when you grew up was a missionary," my sister reminded me as I prepared to enter God's call on my life. I must have been about eleven or maybe twelve when dreams of serving God on the mission field first entered my mind. Mr. Aaron and Mrs. Jean Boeker were missionaries to rural south-central Louisiana. As a child, I didn't know they were missionaries, all I knew was they were an older white couple who came to my church every Tuesday after school for Bible school and the first week of every summer for Vacation Bible School (VBS).

I would skip and halfway run to the Greater First Baptist Church (formerly First Baptist Church) just down the sidewalk from my house. Mr. Boeker would make his rounds throughout the segregated neighborhoods, gathering Black kids in their olive green and white Suburban. They would keep me and the other children in my community mesmerized with the Bible stories illustrated on a flannel board. Straining our young voices to sing in Mrs. Boeker's high soprano key, we would sing hymn after hymn. There was always a quiz to test our knowledge of the Bible stories and the books of the Bible. Getting rewarded for memorizing Bible verses was so much fun! Picking a prize from the shoe box covered with construction paper was the best part. Vacation Bible School was the hottest thing going for kids in small-town Louisiana.

I had not yet turned thirteen when I said yes to Mr. and Mrs. Boeker's offer to help them with VBS during the summers. After the morning Vacation Bible School in some little rural Louisiana town, Mr. Boeker would drive the Suburban to the only little local burger joint, and their other helper and I would get out and order our food. Mrs. Boeker would take out the lunch she had prepared for the two of them, and we would enjoy lunch together. I don't know if the Boeker's were always vegetarians, but I never saw them eat meat. As a child this was a bit strange to me, because I didn't even know there were people who didn't eat meat.

I remember the first time I heard of the African continent was on one of those muggy Louisiana summer days. Africa was this faraway place I came to learn about from letters Mrs. Boeker shared during our lunch break between the morning and afternoon VBS. After ordering our lunch, usually a burger, fries, and a thick strawberry shake, the other helper and I would get back in the Suburban to eat with Mr. and Mrs. Boeker. From time to time, Mrs. Boeker pulled out a letter from Ms. Henrietta, who was serving as a missionary in Africa. Captivated by the stories she wrote about the people of Africa and their way of life, I yearned to know more. I fell in love with cultures and language, maps and geography. Ms. Henrietta's letters described her evangelism work there and how people were becoming followers of Jesus.

Some forty years later, in my work as a missionary with Cru, writing newsletters to my ministry partners, I realize Mrs. Boeker was probably reading Ms. Henrietta's newsletter to her supporters and fellow missionaries. It's amazing how life has come full circle. When you travel new roads or break new ground, the memories and images stay with you for a long time. Like many firsts, they leave a permanent impression in your mind.

I remember how I felt setting foot on the motherland, my ancestors' home, for the first time. It was a feeling of knowing and a distinct sense of belonging. I felt like I was coming home. I remember my first experience of dancing and worshiping God with my African brothers and sisters. I felt connected to people who looked like me but did not talk like me, although their French had a familiar sound that I first heard spoken by my grandmother when I was a child. Their smiles were like mine, their laughter was like mine, their rhythm was like mine, or maybe it was the other way around; I was like them. I thought to myself with a knowing that I could not explain: these are my people, I can feel it; these Beninese people are *my* people. Shortly after my return from Benin, my brother's DNA test results would confirm what I already knew.

The dirt roads and dirt yards, with animals scratching around for a morsel of food, were a memory from my past. The okra, the bounty of rice, the beans, and the peas—all dishes I grew up eating—central to my upbringing. The children had well-worn clothes, just enough to cover their little bodies. Some of the old people were bent over and broken from the weight of work and showing wear and tear on their bodily frames. Not more than three generations ago this could have been the images from colored neighborhoods across our country's southern parts. I recognized it, and it spoke to memories from my past.

On the last day of my stay, a soft-spoken African brother from the Fulani tribe said to me, "I'm so glad you came, and I'm so glad to know you." I responded, "Thank you; it is my pleasure." He insisted again in perfect English, "Thank you for coming to Africa." Once again, I assured him, saying, "You are welcome; I'm glad I came."

His response still reverberates in my mind today, "You are the first African American I have ever met." I was so taken aback by his statement. The surprised expression on my face caused him to repeat, "Yes, you are the first African American I have ever met." My heart became sad under the weight of what he said and silently cried out to the Lord, "This should not be; this should not be!" Until then, it had not occurred to me that I was likely the first African American he—and probably most of the others at the training—had ever met.

After I got over the surprise of his comment, I wondered how could that be? How could it be that this outgoing thirty-something-year-old Christian man had never met an African American? I remained puzzled about this until I returned home and shared this farewell encounter with another Cru missionary friend. She was able to connect the dots for me. She was so kind when she explained, "There are so few Black missionaries; you are probably the first African American any of them has ever seen. We need more Black missionaries to go to Africa," she said. "We need more Black missionaries."

She encouraged me to share this with others. Seeing the expression on my face and knowing how emotional I am about the subject of race, she added, "When you are ready, I really think you should share this." This revelation would explain some of the encounters I had while in Africa that left me perplexed. All of the missionaries this third-generation Christian had ever encountered were white. It was more than I could take in. And to think, all this time in my mind's eye, I pictured Ms. Henrietta as a Black woman, and now I realize the likelihood of that being the case is slim. Ms. Henrietta was most likely a white woman.

6

FIRST BLACK
CHEERLEADER

Run, run, run, round off, round off, high kick, high kick, herkie, herkie, high kick, high kick—this was the series of moves it took me to get from one end of the gym floor to the far end where I shouted in my loudest thirteen-year-old voice, "Ready, OK!" It was the spring of 1977 and I was in the eighth grade when I ran for the varsity cheerleader squad. Full of excitement and nervous energy, I performed the chant and then the cheer I had practiced to perfection and exited the gym floor the same way I entered. Run, run, run, round off, round off, high kick, high kick, herkie, herkie, high kick, high kick, back to my spot alongside the next girl in the competition.

Although it was a competition technically, I was only competing against the other six or seven Black girls who had mustered up enough courage to run for the first and only cheerleader spot to be held by a Black girl at Kinder High. I was the youngest to try out. I stayed up late into the night painting "vote for me" campaign signs with catchy slogans that would line the hallways of the school, soliciting the votes of my fellow classmates.

Nine years after desegregation, and finally we would have a Black cheerleader on the squad the next school year. We would also have one Black girl on the rifle team and two Black girls on the flag team. At the time I thought this monumental change that forced the inclusion of Blacks into these coveted all-important high school positions was the result of Title I. But I was wrong.

One day just a few years before my Mother passed away, I was helping Mom find something in the bedroom I occupy when I'm at home in Kinder. I came across a three-hole-punched blue folder with old papers in it with statistics of the number of Black and white students at Kinder High School. On the pages now stained with age were the ratios of each squad, club, team, and organization and the number of positions statistically that Black students should hold.

Before my eyes was a well-thought-out, logical, and practical proposal promoting Black students' access to participate equally with white students. Back in those days, not one of those positions was held by a Black student. This proposal did not suggest that a Black student occupy one of the current positions but that a position based on ratios should be added to include Black students.

"Mom, what is this?" I exclaimed in amazement at what I was reading.

"What is what?" She returned to see what my excitement was all about.

I flipped the folder back open, handing it to her. "All this time, I thought the reason I was the first Black cheerleader was because of Title I."

"Oh no," Mom responded to my misinformation. "Me, and I think Mrs. Braxton, and I don't remember who else, but we did our homework"—which I was now holding in my hand—"and one morning we marched into Lester Armand's office and made our case. We spelled it all out for him, and he said OK, and that was it."

"Just like that," I said, surprised. "No pushback, no argument."

"Yes, just like that. We had the data and Black-to-white ratios to support what we were asking for, and he agreed. It was a short meeting," Mom said, "and it was done."

I was so proud of my mom that day I could have kissed her whole face, but instead, tears welled up in my eyes, and she knew I was proud of her and the others for standing up for us and being willing to speak up for us to be allowed to participate just like the white kids. And to think that neither Mom nor Dad had ever shared this with my siblings and me!

Change, significant change, happened just like that. I say just like that, but it took years of finding out and learning the ins and outs of the school system in place after desegregation. Mom and Mrs. Irene Henry were the first Black teachers' aides at Kinder High School under the newly implemented Federal Title I Program. This funding came with strings attached. It required a certain number of school jobs, and not just janitors and lunchroom workers, had to be held by Blacks in order to receive this funding.

After being on the inside and seeing how things operated and decisions were made, it became obvious that the Black kids did not stand a chance of being cheerleaders or anything else under the current way of doing things. So parents and teachers took a stand for their kids to be included in a system that was sure to continue to exclude them if it remained the way it was.

I remember overhearing my parents' conversations expressing their frustration with the way things were—the inability for us to participate. I do remember Mom and Dad advocating for us when it was necessary. They didn't always win, but they made sure they were heard. They didn't always like the results, but that didn't stop them from standing up for us.

Progress was slow, but wins along the way kept us all advocating for rights that were held tightly and had to be pried out one by one. This struggle has been constant and deliberate on both sides: whites not wanting to relinquish what they are accustomed to having and Blacks insisting on being treated fairly and given opportunities to advance and be a part of the American dream.

I look back on the brilliance of this proposal, and it's no wonder Mr. Armand agreed without hesitation. They were not asking for a position held by a white child to be given to a Black child; they were asking to add a place for a Black child so that we could participate as well.

The cheerleader squad went from six to seven cheerleaders, the rifle team went from six to seven, and the flag core increased from twelve to fourteen girls. By then Black kids were already playing sports with the white kids, but the girls were essentially locked out of non-athletic activities due to the status quo or them essentially being popularity contests. But that year in the eighth grade, back in 1977, everything changed in this young kid's life.

Becoming the first Black cheerleader at Kinder High School would change the trajectory of my life, literally. My summers that were once filled gallivanting all over southwest Louisiana with the Boekers teaching five-year-olds about Jesus would give way to summers filled with long hours of cheerleader practice in preparation for cheerleader camp and the upcoming football season. I did not look back at this fork in the road in my young life with the seriousness that it warranted until forty years later.

Dear Lord,

I thank You for parents like Mom and Dad and teachers who stood up for us. I thank You for Lester Armand and people like him who opened doors without hesitation. I know there are countless more who courageously moved racial equality forward. Thank you for the unsung heroes. May we step up now that it is our turn to be brave and courageous in the face of inequality and unfair treatment of any people. Lord, may we stand in the gap for those without a voice or whose voices have been just a whisper for too long. In Jesus' name. Amen.

CHAPTER

7

THAT'S JUST THE WAY IT WAS

We sat on the hard cold floor in the hallway in front of the school auditorium—all seven of us sitting in a circle with a tiny box in the middle. The next year would be my senior year in high school and my fourth year on the cheerleader squad. Legs crossed we each contemplated the instructions we were given for electing next year's head cheerleader.

There we were, young and eager and making a decision that would set the hierarchy for the following year. Or was this still a part of the popularity contest that a cheerleader competition is when voted on by the student body? Either way, it was a choice we would have to live with through the fall football season and into the playoffs, followed by basketball season both on and off the school bus and right through the spring track season.

Each of us held a small slip of paper, barely large enough for a first and last name. Leaning in one by one, each girl dropped her tightly folded piece of paper into the little box that now held all of our attention. It didn't take long to cast our votes; certainly not as long as one would think for a memory that has lasted a lifetime in my mind.

I would be the only senior on the squad—with the most seniority and the most experience. But I was also Black, the only Black. One Black and six white cheerleaders. Some were new to the squad, and some were reelected by the student body. But not one of those cheerleaders voted for me. Not one!

When I learned that not one of them voted for me, I was shocked but not surprised. I didn't fully understand, but I knew a vote for me would take courage, given the way it was in my small town. They would never put me in charge of the squad. They would not have me calling the shots and making the decisions. These young ladies could not see me as their leader, but the cheerleader coach could. She had witnessed my hard work and perseverance over the years I was on the squad. She had experienced my character and dedication on and off the court, as she was also my basketball coach. She knew me to be honest and fair and watched me collect All-Tournament Player and Most Outstanding Sportsmanship Awards. And she knew I deserved to be the head cheerleader.

I was not elected by the cheerleaders that day, but my cheerleader coach chose me. When my cheerleader coach announced that there would be two head cheerleaders and that we would co-lead the squad, I realized that my peers did not elect me, but my leader had chosen me, and that was enough for me; it had to be.

I'm still friends with the beautiful co-head cheerleader. We reminisce about those days of endless practices when we climbed on top of one another, making the tallest pyramid a seven-person squad could build. I don't want to sugarcoat it, but when I look back on it now I can see how it benefited both of us to co-lead. She would be the only senior on the squad the following year, and co-leading served as excellent preparation for the coming year. Even now, when we see each other, we revisit the hours the squad spent in my backyard together, working toward perfection. We were bent on winning every award in the competition. We were good! And we still are good, she and I.

As I'm writing this, I stop and retrieve my high school letter-jacket from the top rung of my closet where all of my coats hang. Concealed in a white plastic covering, it is the oldest of them all by far. I almost miss it and begin to grow uneasy about where it could be. I bring it into the room where I'm writing and take my seat, uncovering the short black coat covered in black and gold patches. I drape it over my lap and begin to finger the patches, each of them representing hours and hours of morning and evening practices and years of my young life.

The "Big K" on the front of my jacket sports five stripes for the five years I played on the high school basketball team. The same coach also coached my junior high team. She noticed my ability and let me begin practicing and then playing with the junior varsity team. These five strips represent thousands of layups, rebounds, and countless free-throw shots. The patch shaped like a megaphone sports four stripes for my years on the cheerleader squad from 1978–81 with the embroidered letters, "Head Cheerleader."

Each shoulder displays the numbers of my basketball jersey, 40 for home games and 13 for away games. Under the black and gold #13 is a round patch with lettering, "Outstanding Offensive Player 77–78," and another one recognizing my presence on the Homecoming Court in 1980. Under the #40 patch is one that reads, "Miss Black Allen Parish 1978" and "Swimsuit Queen." As I read this one, I start tearing up and I began searching my heart for the reason behind the tears.

Although this was a happy time in my life, looking back on it reveals another layer of my story. These were times when Blacks and whites only intermingled at school and in a few workplaces because of the recent years of desegregation. These were times when my aunts and great-aunts worked as domestics cleaning the homes of white people with means, like those depicted in Kathryn Stockett's book *The Help*. Back in these days, my great uncles farmed in fields of wealthy landowners growing rice and soybeans, worked as janitors, and did jobs white men did not want to do.

Later, I would help make up the first graduating class at Kinder High with Black students who had never attended the all-Black school. The white school was all we knew. The same could be said of my white classmates. They had never gone to a segregated school either.

Recognizing the reality of the times represented by the word *Black* on my patch reminded me that we were a part of the school, but not always an equal part. We attended the same school as the white kids, but we were by no means having the same experience. Every accomplishment had its struggles and sometimes demands. Many advancements came because we had gently and gingerly made room for ourselves. The reality is that back in those days, there was no way the Black girls were going to compete in the same beauty pageant as the white girls. It was utterly inconceivable back then. That's just the way it was in my hometown.

Depending on where you are from, I'm sure it wasn't much different in your hometown. Small-town America was much the same across the country in the 1960s and 1970s. There may have been marginal differences between the cities and rural areas of the country, but the tension between how we experience equality in liberties *for all* and the denial of access *to all* was happening in varying degrees nationwide. While some progress has been made, we are a country of people who see color loudly and vividly. Unfortunately, we see our color differences with our eyes and our heads and not with our hearts.

As you reflect on this scene or a similar scene in your own life, whom do you identify with the most? Do you remember a time when you had to be courageous and advocate for a person different from you? Can you describe a time when a person you worked with was looked over for a promotion or an advancement because of their ethnicity? Did you do anything about it? Would you do anything differently now? Questions like these help us search within ourselves and get at the heart of these matters, which is what motivates our actions and how they play out in our lives and the lives of others.

Jill, one of my younger sisters, recounts, "It was everything to me when you and Rosie let me and Tammy cheer with the squad at one of the football games." Honestly, I didn't remember that until she began telling the story full of excitement and laughter. She described it as one of her fondest childhood memories. "You remember," she said, "we had on those little cheerleader uniforms, and we were so excited to be up there with the big cheerleaders." Jill and Tammy (one of my younger cousins) were taking gymnastics, tap dancing, and ballet classes. Rosie, our head cheerleader that year, was an instructor at the dance studio and worked with Jill and Tammy on their flips and tumbling. What an extraordinary opportunity afforded two young Black girls in those days! Now more than ever, I realize the investments and sacrifices my mom and dad made for us kids.

"Jill, who made the uniforms?" I inquired.

"Mom and Aunt Lula made our uniforms." I could then picture the small black, gold, and white uniforms.

"How old were you then?" I asked as I began counting the years backward. Jill is seven years younger than me, and her dream of being a cheerleader was wrapped up in my dream, which was playing out in her young life. "I was in the sixth grade, so I would have been about eleven-years-old or so," Jill calculated. Jill would go on to be a junior high school cheerleader. (My younger sisters, Jameeka and Kayla, were also Kinder High School cheerleaders).

Some five years after I graduated from high school, Jill, with the encouragement of Rosie and the beautiful co-head cheerleader, crossed the color line into the white pageant. After years of having separate pageants, crowning Black queens and white queens for years, the progression to unify the pageant finally happened. Can you imagine the courage it took? I can.

It is the story of our lives. Going where you are not necessarily welcomed, daring to get your feelings hurt along the way, knowing that not everyone is going to meet your courage with open arms and smiles. Having to ignore the sneers and the sly comments was commonplace. Rolling eyes and turned backs were gestures you might as well get used to. It took a made-up mind and plenty of encouragement and affirmation at home to keep coming back for more neglect and shunning from some of your peers and sometimes adults too. But my sister was beautiful and talented, and there was no denying it. After all, this was not a popularity contest; it was a beauty pageant and talent competition, and the judges rewarded her with first runner-up. No, she didn't get a crown, but we were so proud of her that she might as well have. She had done what no one else had ever done in my town. In 1986, she entered the white pageant and won first runner-up.

Another decade and a half later, my youngest sister Kayla broke another glass ceiling in 2002, when she became the first Black young lady to be crowned Miss Kinder. What I didn't realize at the time is that we had been preparing Kayla her whole life for that moment. She took dance and piano lessons as a young girl, not to mention all of the church activities she was privy to. She was an extension of all our dreams and aspirations.

There I was with Kayla in the high school band room. It was adjacent to the auditorium's stage and doubled as the makeshift dressing room for the pageant's contestants. We had staked out our little section of the room and laid out all of Kayla's carefully selected outfits and shiny accessories. Accounting for every detail, we lined up earrings, necklaces, shoes, and rhinestone barrettes in the order of the evening's competition.

We agreed on a stunning rhinestone-studded hot pink satin gown for Kayla that perfectly complemented her flawless complexion. It fit like a glove, showing off her perfectly curved, athletic physique. Those years on the basketball court were paying off. She was stunning. A real show-stopper! The other young ladies could not come close to her poise and stage presence under the single spotlight that made her sparkle. Of course, these are the words of a biased big sister.

But the big question was, *Will she be awarded the crown?* Was Kinder ready for its first Black Miss Kinder? Everyone in my family and half of the Black community were there holding our breath and praying. I didn't know if we could handle her not being crowned queen, like when Jill placed first runner-up fifteen years before. Every time Kayla stepped out on the stage, we cheered her on as if our lives depended on it. Oh yes, we were proud of her, and we were loud. She had the support of her community, and there was no denying it was time.

It was down to two finalists. The fourth, third, and second-place winners were already named and holding their trophies, and Kayla was one of two still standing in the finalists circle. One would be queen, and the other would be the first runner-up. It was tight. It was a nail-biter. "And the new Miss Kinder 2002 is Kayla

Williams," the mistress of ceremony dramatically announced, ending our suspense. We could hardly believe our ears! Our eyes gushed with tears of joy as we experienced the sweet flavor of this long-sought-after history-making moment. We cheered and hugged and cried and hugged some more before racing onto the stage to congratulate and embrace our little sister. She had done it! Kinder's first *Black* Miss Kinder.

As we passed by the judges' table to thank them after the pageant, each judge had such high compliments for Kayla. They were all smiles. They had been a part of making history in my small hometown. The scales of subjective partiality had finally fallen off—or at least blinked. This was the moment that a young Black girl could be seen as their queen. We celebrated her, and later Kayla helped other Black girls see themselves as queen material. Until recently, her full-length portrait still graced the wall in the hallway of our family home. Just a glimpse of the picture as I pass through the house, and I'd get all caught up in the moment again.

Kayla said, "For a few years, LaToya and I sponsored someone in the pageant to help with the cost to participate." LaToya received coaching and encouragement from Kayla the years before LaToya was crowned Miss Kinder. Now LaToya Tunwar is the first Black woman on the Kinder City Council. I would venture to say that their confidence and can-do spirit were born back in their days as young ladies coached and inspired by family and friends who could see the possibilities in them long before they recognized themselves.

When I was a cheerleader some forty years ago, it took lots of extra money for uniforms and outfits for cheerleader camps and competitions. In my case, it took two parents making a decent income to support my childhood dreams and the aspirations of my seven siblings. My parents sowed heavily into us in encouragement, physical support, their presence, and financial sacrifice. But first and foremost, it was the opportunities and hard work on the part of my mom and dad that afforded us the ability to participate in the American dream.

Every parent wants the best for his or her children. African American parents are no different. But when the doors are closed tightly, and access is not granted, hopes and dreams die. Aspirations of a better future wither away. Sure, many people of color can and do claw their way up the ladder and out of poverty, but currently, Blacks are overrepresented in poverty and inequalities still persist. Can you see the hopelessness in the eyes of children of color? When "pay to play" is how to gain entry into children's activities during their early formative years, you quickly realize that partiality is also green.

Are you moved to do something to make a difference? Are you willing to ask yourself probing questions like, "Why aren't there more people of color at my kid's school or on my kid's team or squad? Why aren't more people of color represented? Why aren't there more people of color on my job? What is my Christian duty to see that all people are included and granted access? Is it good enough that my kids have access while others stand on the sidelines wanting in? Where can I help? What can I do? How can I change what is right before me? What do I have the power to change for the better? Could I give a scholarship for a kid to be involved? Could I pay for their uniforms? Could I give a kid a ride to and from practice? What could I do, and when will I do it?"

Dear Lord,

Please forgive me for not seeing what is right before me in Black, white, and green. Please forgive me for trudging ahead and not looking back to see if others are making progress. Please forgive me for not noticing that the road I traveled is obstructed with roadblocks. Lord, help me do my part to see that all people, but especially the under-resourced, are granted access and the opportunity to achieve. We should not put limits on opportunities. You are a limitless God. Please help me and others that I serve alongside find ways to include more people of color. Dear Lord, thank You for convicting me of my passive attitude toward the plight of others. Please, open my eyes to see the needs of others, and help me do a better job of responding to those concerns going forward. In Jesus' name, I pray in all sincerity. Amen.

Reflection

If a thought stirs your feelings or a question resonates with you, I invite you to reflect on why and maybe even get a journal and write about something that may have happened in the past. I encourage you to practice examining your heart in the presence of God before continuing your unity in Christ journey.

_____

_____

_____

_____

_____

_____

_____

_____

_____

_____

_____

_____

_____

_____

_____

_____

_____

_____

CHAPTER

8

WRITING ON
THE WALL

A third, a third, a third. By my rough estimate, approximately a third of the class of 1981 would go to college after graduation, a third would go to a branch of service, and a third would get jobs and get married. I was in the latter third, marrying my high school boyfriend the following year. After several years of marriage, seeing the writing on the wall, I would sum up my deteriorating and destined-to-fail marriage this way, "'I've spent five years of my life, and all I have to show for it is a son,' or I can later say, 'I've spent twenty years of my life and all I have to show for it is a son.' Either way, the result would be the same." This revelation gave me the clarity I needed to move on and start over.

Before my divorce was final, I moved to Houston with my son and took the first job I was offered. My godmother had secured me a position with her employer, working at a furniture company. One day after work, I took my son to an audition for a children's commercial, and the talent agent asked me if I had ever thought about modeling. The idea piqued my curiosity, and I thought it could provide another source of income. Although it never produced a substantial income from a commercial here or a runway show there, the modeling studio served as the place where I would meet my husband of now thirty-four years. He was working, raising his two daughters, and attending modeling classes, hoping to make some extra money eventually. The fact is, neither of us had the height typically associated with someone having a lucrative modeling career, but I guess it served its purpose; we found each other.

Sitting in the hairstylist chair, getting ready for a photo shoot, I saw this handsome guy strolling past the floor-to-ceiling glass window with long, confident strides. I asked the stylist, "Who is that?" She replied, "Oh, that's Chester." We moved on to another topic, which was the end of the conversation about Chester. It was very out of character for me to inquire about a guy in such a way. But until then, I had not seen any Black men at the agency.

A couple of weeks later, I was invited to join the still-life mannequin class. And guess who else was there? Chester. This was my second time seeing him, but my first time meeting him. We were to participate in a still-life mannequin fashion show at a mall in the suburbs north of Houston. I was one of four Black students in the class, two ladies and two guys. Being new to Houston, way before navigation systems were a thing, I suggested exchanging phone numbers just in case we (mainly I) needed help finding the place. Chester took it upon himself to use my phone number for a reason other than why it had been provided. He called me one evening to talk, and the rest is history. I'm sure he has a different version of this story, but he will have to write his book to tell his account.

In the summer of 1988, I got my first break into the airline industry. I responded to an ad in the *Houston Chronicle* newspaper announcing that Continental Airlines was looking for flight attendants. Being a flight attendant was something I had fantasized about years before so I could travel, but living in Louisiana did not afford me that opportunity. Imagine my excitement when I was selected to attend the upcoming flight attendant training.

In the meantime, Chester had landed a job in Pennsylvania, and one evening (over the phone, mind you), he informed me and asked if I would move to Pennsylvania with him. I quickly let him know he was getting a little ahead of himself. He agreed, and we resolved to talk about it in person. Well, he proposed that evening, and I decided I would move to Pennsylvania with him.

After passing several rigorous exams, I graduated, was certified, and was assigned Newark, New Jersey, as my station. What a culture shock for this small-town girl from Louisiana, but I made the best of it along with others from my class stationed there. I loved being a flight attendant and serving people in the friendly skies, but I didn't particularly like the lifestyle that caused me to be away from home and my son. Continental's headquarters was in Houston, and Houston was their largest hub, so I hadn't seriously entertained being stationed elsewhere.

Later the following year, Chester and I married and moved our blended young family to Pennsylvania. I was blessed to be able to transfer to ground services as a ticket agent with Continental in Pennsylvania. I worked for them for two days before I got a call from USAir, the dominant carrier in the northeast at the time, to come to work for them. This allowed me to be home with my family and bond with my new husband. After a couple of years working with USAir at the Philadelphia airport, God answered our prayers to leave the harsh winters for the climate we were accustomed to and transfer back to Houston to be closer to our beloved parents in Texas and Louisiana.

It was then that I began to take notice of God's hand in my life, both in terms of my career and His provisions for our family. It was as if God was showing me the writing on the wall at each transition and opening the door for a new job just before the old one ended. This would happen again and again throughout my twenty years in the airline industry and fifteen years in Christian ministry.

My earliest memory of being acutely aware of God preparing me in advance for what was coming was when my job with USAir ended. My district manager had already taken a job with another airline carrier, and I was the only person in the office for several months. I knew it was just a matter of time before the company would have to do something, as they had yet to replace the district manager. I began looking for a job and found one that took me outside of the travel industry for a couple of years. I accepted the job and wrote my resignation letter to advise USAir that I would be leaving after two weeks.

I arrived at the office that Friday morning with the resignation letter in my briefcase. Shortly after I opened the office, I received a call from the district manager from the Dallas area, saying she was at the airport in Houston and was coming to the office to visit me. I surmised what the visit was about but sat tight until she arrived to inform me that they were closing the Houston sales office. I never said a word about my resignation letter sitting in my briefcase at my feet. I just listened as she explained my final compensation and the health benefits that would provide coverage for me and my family until the very day my benefits started with my new company.

I don't remember if the office closed immediately that day or if I worked the next two weeks, but watching God specifically take care of me and my family gave me a glimpse of God's love for me. This intentional and apparent act of love and provision inspired a higher level of trusting God with my life and everything that concerns me. He has orchestrated for me to grow from one job to another without any lag in between, elevating me each step throughout my career.

Over the decades, God has also graciously given me favor with men and women throughout every aspect of my life. In sharing vignettes from my story, I set out to share the complexities and nuances of an African American from my lived experience. Not all have been unpleasant as my accounts in this book may suggest; in fact, most have been extremely good.

I have enjoyed many cross-cultural relationships and am honored to have an especially diverse group of friends from various backgrounds, some of whom you will hear from in the coming chapters. I have been so blessed to collect friends along the way, some of whom I still enjoy today. As I encourage making new and lasting friendships, it reminds me of one of my favorite poems, "New Friends and Old Friends," by Joseph Parry.

Make new friends, but keep the old;
Those are silver, these are gold.
New-made friendships, like new wine,
Age will mellow and refine.
Friendships that have stood the test—
Time and change—are surely best;
Brow may wrinkle, hair grow gray,
Friendship never knows decay.
For 'mid old friends, tried and true,
Once more we our youth renew.

But old friends, alas! may die,
New friends must their place supply.
Cherish friendship in your breast—
New is good, but old is best;
Make new friends, but keep the old;
Those are silver, these are gold.

One of my old friends is a special lady gifted to me years ago. She and her husband were ministry partners. On the flight to visit them, I was praying to God. I mentioned to God that I had heard people say that when we get to heaven, there will be a room full of presents we had not received because we hadn't asked God for them. I admitted to God that I didn't know if it was true, but I asked Him to surprise me with a present today. I also asked God to make sure I knew the gift was from Him.

I got off the plane, rented a car, and went about my day, forgetting about my prayer. I drove to their home on the outskirts of town, where their farm was. She and I had talked on the phone multiple times but had not yet met in person. She showed me around her home, pointing out pictures on the walls and things she collected and telling me stories about her family. She then showed me the beautifully appointed guest room where I would sleep, all decked out in blue. Lastly, we turned and left the guest room, and she pointed out stairs that led to the basement/storm shelter and invited me to go down there in the morning for my quiet time with God if I would like. We visited some more over supper, talking about recipes, travel, family traditions, and what seemed like everything under the sun. Our conversation continued over dessert, cleaning the kitchen, and finally going to bed.

After getting dressed the following day, I took her up on her offer. I went downstairs to the one-room finished basement and got comfortable in the oversized leather chair that was the room's crowning jewel. I got quiet, and a *knowing* came over me, making it abundantly clear that she was the gift that God had given me. With tears in my eyes, I thanked God for this most amazing gift of a new friend. I shared it with her over breakfast that morning, and she was overjoyed, too. Realizing that God thought of her as a gift let me know how special she was, and appreciating that God would bless me with this gift of a new friend overwhelmed me. God knows how much I treasure the gift of friendship, and the more diverse the better. Since then, understanding that each friend is from God, I treasure them even more.

CHAPTER
9

FIRST IN LINE

The clerk's eyes averted from mine as she put the "Closed" sign away under the counter. Looking right past me, she opened her window. The clerk asked the lady standing just off to my right, "May I help you?" as their eyes locked. I tore my eyes away from the clerk and glanced over my shoulder at the lady who arrived shortly after I did. "Sure," she said as she stepped past me, handing the clerk her papers. Several people had meandered into the lobby and were also waiting for the staff to return from lunch.

It's as if I'm invisible. Appalled, I stood there with my mouth open in disbelief, rejecting the thoughts running through my head. Maybe she didn't see me. No, she saw me! It was obvious that I was first in line. She finished the transaction, the lady gathered her papers, and while the lady was shoving them in her purse, the white clerk looked up, making eye contact with me. "Next," she said as I stepped forward. I'm always shocked and sometimes even outraged when this happens. And just as I can't predict when the next occurrence will be, I cannot predict how I will respond.

This time I was seething, but I fought back my anger, handing her my paperwork. She was cordial enough as she waited on me, but no amount of niceties would undo the feeling in my gut that stayed with me well into the evening. Being overlooked, dismissed, unseen—call it what you want—always leaves me with an awful feeling that I find hard to shake. Somehow it seeps into my subconscious and affects me in ways that are hard to describe. After the anger subsides, an unhealthy loathing sets in.

From my point of view, I had been offended and possibly even taken advantage of. I tried to give the clerk the benefit of the doubt. "Well, maybe she didn't see me." "Maybe she couldn't tell that I was first in line." But it was obvious that I was first; I was clearly in front of her. And even if it wasn't clear to the clerk, the lady next to me knew I was first. I was standing there when she came in the door. She nodded when our eyes met. I guess the awful pit I felt in my stomach was compounded by the fact that it took both of them, the clerk and the lady, to perpetuate this offense.

The lady could have easily said to the clerk, "She's first," but she didn't. Instead, she just whizzed past me, took the privilege extended to her, and went on about her day, leaving me to feel slighted, dismissed, and awful at the reminder that some people still see me as less than the white person standing next to me.

I probably wouldn't be telling you this story if it had only happened once in my life. But I'm sorry to say that this scene has been a recurring event in my life over many years. And I wish I could report that this is something of the distant past, but that would be wishful thinking. Thankfully, it doesn't happen as often as it used to, but it does still happen to me from time to time.

And for that reason, you would think I would get used to it, but somehow it always catches me off guard, leaving me with the same awful, sick-to-my-stomach feeling.

I must say that surprisingly, I have had this scene play out differently, but it's not because I did anything different. It's because the person next in line was gracious enough to say, "She was here first," gesturing for me to take my rightful place at the counter, forcing the clerk to acknowledge me. My face brightens to a broad smile and a soft *thank you*. Then I'm left with a feeling that *all is well* in the world, and I'm able to ignore the offense of the clerk and dwell on the person who did the right thing, righting the wrong that was being perpetrated on me, which could only happen if she participated.

There is yet another way this scene can play out, and I must say, I've been a witness and participant in all three scenarios. Looking right past me, the clerk asks the lady standing just off to my right, "May I help you?" I tear my eyes away from the clerk and glance over my shoulder at the lady who arrived after I did. Then my eyes dart back at the clerk, and I assert, "I was here first," moving toward the counter with my papers in hand. There's usually no protest from the lady behind me or the others waiting; there is just silence. I let my response, "I was here first," reverberate and echo in the silence. This scenario leaves me with the same *yucky* feeling as the first scenario. I'm not sure why it still leaves me with a bad taste in my mouth, but it does, so much so that I avoid this scene, if I can catch myself, choosing to let the other customer go first and not making a fuss. I've matured in this area, having learned that this outcome leaves me feeling pretty good inside too.

Shortly after the Lord gave me the inspiration for this chapter, it occurred to me that while this has happened to me numerous times, I had never actually talked to anyone about it before, Black or white. But human nature tells me that if this happens to me as often as it does, it must also be happening to my fellow sisters and brothers of color. I just assumed they were also receiving the same treatment from time to time.

So, one day I decided to inquire of people of color to see if this had ever happened to them, starting with my husband. Without hesitation, he shot back, "Well, yeah!" I asked, "More than once?" and he said, "Sure, it happens all the time." I was not surprised in the least. The thought that this happens to someone I love and who is so respectful of others tore at my heart. Since then, I have asked dozens of people of color this same question, and I am not shocked by my findings. I no longer assume but have confirmed that this act of microaggression is being perpetrated on people of color one person at a time, day in and day out, and it was not just my personal experience.

I look back over my life, and I remember a time when this treatment by a white person would cause me to become indignant and demand to be recognized and treated fairly. Then as I grew in maturity, I realized that my reaction only added another layer of disdain in the hearts of the offenders, because while I may have forced them to wait on me first, it did nothing to accomplish the result I wanted, and that was to be seen and respected. We all have the choice to sow discord or goodwill. Every day, opportunities present themselves. We have to ask ourselves, "Which one am I promoting, discord or goodwill?"

How does what I've shared make you feel? Do you remember ever being in a similar situation or witnessing something like this happening? What part did you play as the scene unfolded? How did that make you feel then, and how do you feel about it now? How do you think it made the other person feel?

Thank God, these experiences don't negate the countless hundreds and thousands of times I am met with gladness. Nor does it speak to the kindness I am shown every day by people who are loving, courteous, and decent. I am naturally a cheery person who smiles all the time. As one of my Master's Program for Women sisters describes me, "You are the smile in the room." So, when a smile meets a smile, it is as if, like a red carpet, a *welcome mat* has just been rolled out in between. Be that welcome mat who meets people with a smile.

> *Dear Lord,*
>
> *Please give me the ability to put myself in another person's shoes. I know in my fallen state, it is not natural to empathize with others, but with Your help I can consider the feelings of others. Please help me be sensitive to what others may be experiencing, for this is the beginning of empathy. Lord, please help me know what to do in these situations. Thank You, Lord, for exposing me to the plight of people who look different from me. And help me respond according to Your Word. In Jesus' name. Amen.*

10

MY FIRST VAN GOGH

My first teachers were my mom and dad. They were giants in my life. Just like a full-grown adult towers over a toddler learning to take her first steps, my parents have always been giants in my life, teaching me how to love the Lord (who first loved us) and to navigate this less than equal life that we were born into.

Mom was the smartest, quickest thinker I knew. And there I was soaking up everything she knew, from baking and preserving to sewing, to her way around the kitchen, and her decorative flair. Mom always seemed to have it all together. There was never a time in my life when I doubted whether my mom knew what she was doing. She exuded unshakable confidence that was uncommon for a woman of color of her era, and it showed in everything she did.

I would have only been four and a half years old when

> *on April 11, 1968, seven days after King's assassination, Congress finally passed the Fair Housing Act. The Fair Housing Act protects buyers and renters of housing from discrimination by sellers, landlords, or financial institutions and makes it unlawful for those entities to refuse to rent, sell, or provide financing for a dwelling based on factors other than an individual's financial resources.[1]*

Mom and Dad had one of the first brick homes built in the Nixon addition section of town, on the same lot as our previous home. Lenders began making loans more widely available to Blacks after new legislation finally passed in the 1970s. The law required that private lenders provide statistics of race, gender, and location of applicants to the Federal Housing Authority (FHA), founded in 1934. When Mom found out about these longer termed mortgages at lower interest rates, she quickly figured out how to apply, and their loan got approved. Then she went about telling everybody she could and showing them how to fill out the paperwork and get qualified for the low-interest housing loan.

In the summer of 1972, we moved into our three-bedroom, two-bath home on C Street, later named Kings Drive. That is when Mom's designer instinct reached its peak, revealing her appreciation for art and the finer things in life. Even as a child, waking up to paintings of Gainsborough's *Blue Boy* and the answer to it, *Pinkie,* by the famous artist Thomas Lawrence, shaped in my mind and ambitions in ways only a child psychologist could

---

1 - https://www.britannica.com/topic/Fair-Housing-Act

explain. Who can calculate the impact van Gogh's *Sunflowers* hanging in our living room had on me?

"It's not her fault she grew up with pictures on her wall," my sister-in-law expressed in defense of me one day. Until then, I had never really appreciated how much pictures on the walls had shaped me. And these were not just any pictures; they were replicas of some of the most notable artwork in history. The original art hangs on museum walls while the famous artists who painted them continue to live through their renowned artwork. The silent impressions were unknowingly etching echoes of endless possibilities in my young imagination. All the while, the world outside of my walls was screaming, "No, not yet."

In some ways nowadays, it feels like the present-day screams are screeching, "No not yet, and maybe never." Was this American dream intended for me too? Was it ever meant for me and my people to wholly enjoy? Or were we to just look on at the enjoyment of others' laughter and bliss? What measure of my joy would be tolerated before someone said, "Now that's enough; you are taking what's ours"? Or, "You are getting too big for your britches," as the folks would say in the olden days.

When a new pair of three-dollar shoes can get you fired from your housekeeping job, you know you have overstepped your bounds. Didn't you see that this act on your part was going to get you put back in your place? My grandmother Eola, in the French Creole accent of her mother's first language, warned her eldest daughter, "Don't you wear dos new shoes to work, you gon' get fired." But no, she wouldn't listen. She pranced right into the large wood-frame house in her new shoes.

One glance at the shiny new shoes was all it took to raise the emotions and response of the lady of the house. "Well, if you can afford new shoes like that, you don't need this job. Don't bother coming back tomorrow." Whether it's van Gogh on the wall or getting fired from your much-needed job because of a pair of new shoes, our surroundings continually shape our lives. We are shaped and molded by those around us, some loving and some not so much. How we allow them to transform our existence is left to be decided. You choose if it will break you or inspire you. You decide to give each experience purpose, making you smarter and teaching you coping skills invaluable to your survival.

Little did I know that reproductions of sunflowers and priceless portraits of aristocrats who look nothing like me would shape my world and future aspirations. They would shape how I saw myself in the world. Each item was placed there by my mother, whose dreams and opportunities were limited by "whites only" signs and mandates to hire only one Black. Every sconce, lace tablecloth, or perfectly appointed room of the house that looked like it could have been in the *Better Homes and Gardens* magazine was Mom's way of painting a better future for her children.

I think of my mom and dad and people like them and marvel at all they accomplished with the limited resources and measured opportunities parsed out to them during our country's desegregation era. Make no bones about it; my parents did the best they could with the hand they were dealt. But I often wonder how much farther they could have gone if all people were seen as they were created—all equal in the eyes of God. "For there is no partiality with God" (Rom. 2:11 NKJV).

Even with all this preparation and being reared by optimistic parents who persisted during a challenging era in our country, I was not prepared to hear, "We don't have any more apartments available," from the leasing agent.

"What do you mean you don't have any more apartments?" my flight attendant friend snapped back.

"We don't have any more apartments to lease," the agent repeated with a little more firmness.

"Some of our flight attendant friends told us to come here because you had apartments available," we rebutted.

"Well, we don't have anymore." And that was that.

In the South you know your place, and the color lines were clearly drawn. But here we are in anytown, New Jersey, being turned away from leasing an apartment we know is available. We drove back to the apartment we shared with our flight attendant friends, where their packing had already begun, and relayed the experience of being turned away and denied leasing an apartment. We thought we were shocked; our white flight attendant friends were even more shocked at what we told them. "Sure, they have apartments to lease. We were just there, and they have apartments available," they insisted.

In their disbelief, two of the other white girls decided to go to the apartment complex and see if they would be able to lease an apartment. Sure enough, the next day, when they inquired about an available apartment, they were offered an application to lease that day. They revealed, "Our Black friends were just here and were told that you don't have any apartments available," to which the leasing agent replied something like, "We didn't, but now we do."

They hurried back to report this appalling, despicable practice they could not believe existed at all, let alone in 1989. This infuriated our white friends. "I would report this to someone," one of them said. And believe me, we wanted to. "That's discrimination. I would go back up there and tell them what just happened and demand an apartment," another girl piped in. "Let's go back up there together and expose them, because this is not fair," another friend piled on. But coming from our Black experiences, the three of us knew all this was futile.

And furthermore, who had the time to fight the system? We had to report for duty in the next couple of days. It would be much easier just to find a place to lease that didn't practice this type of discrimination. I remember thinking I had experienced subtle and some not-so-subtle discrimination in my life, but this was blatant discrimination that could not be denied, and they didn't seem to care enough to disguise what they were doing. Our white friends were appalled and angry that this happened to us. We were angry and hurt that this happened to us, and we were sure it happened to others too.

Imagine where we would be in our country's growth and unity if indeed everyone were treated as equals. How would our collective and individual experiences be different from what plays out in our country then and even during this current era? Make no mistake, our children and grandchildren will look back on this time in history just like we pore over the history of the 1950s and 1960s and yes even the 1970s. I pray to our Lord that at minimum we Christians pass the test and will not have to go around this divisive mountain one more time.

> *Dear Lord,*
>
> *Please help us to see Your heart and Your love for everyone You created and treat one another as we would like to be treated. May we not be envious of one another and despise the blessings and accomplishments You want to bestow on Your children. May we hurt when another hurts and rejoice when another sister or brother in Christ rejoices. May we see ourselves as one family, as we are all one in Christ. Lord, will You create in us new sight that sees what You see in every person? Sweet Jesus, please help us; we obviously cannot do this alone. Amen.*

CHAPTER

11

FIRST INTERVIEW

Her face said everything as she rounded the mahogany reception desk. I noticed the surprise on her face, and I realized she had thought I was white. It's not the first time I've seen that expression when a person is faced with the reality that I'm not white. Trying to conceal her surprise, she tugged at the jacket of her business suit and struggled to hold a pleasant countenance. As her facial expressions moved from surprise to a nervous smile, she extended her hand and gave me a firm handshake. She would have sworn that I was white. I returned the smile, and we exchanged pleasantries.

"So nice to meet you," she said.

"And you as well," I responded. It's evident that she had no idea. Would I be at this interview right now if she had?

"Follow me," she beckoned. Trailing close behind her into the small conference room, I took the seat she offered me facing the window. "May I get you some water or coffee?" she asked, still trying to get over the shock of my skin tone.

"Sure, water would be nice," I replied. She walked away and into the breakroom just down the hall for a bottle of water.

Meanwhile, the prayer that had been my request all morning reverberated in my head and heart. "Lord, please let her see me for who I really am, and don't let any prejudices she may have get in the way of her offering me this job. Lord, please cancel out any reservations she may have and give me Your favor!"

I was hoping she was not prejudiced and that her hesitation in the reception area was just her surprise. I'm sad to say that I've seen this look more times than I care to count. Would she be able to put aside her reservations? What were her hesitations founded on? I realized she had the power to say yes or no, and she didn't have to give me any explanation. I felt vulnerable and a little antsy, but I kept my composure and kept praying. It's all I knew how to do.

She returned with a professional politeness, but it was apparent that she was still struggling and arguing with herself over the memory of our phone interview. I could almost see the wheels of her mind in motion, pilfering through the memory of our phone conversation. *There was no indication that I wasn't white.* Our discussion had given her no clues regarding my ethnicity. But clearly, I was not what she imagined me to be when she talked to me on the phone.

I had spoken with her in my most professional, sweet southern voice, careful not to give away my ethnicity with my diction. Answering her questions, "Yes." "Absolutely." "Very well." "Not a problem," as the phone interview went along. Careful to listen and not to get too excited and lose my composure, holding on until the last, "I know exactly where that is. I'll see you there." Putting down the receiver, I shouted, "Yes, thank You, Lord Jesus." I had gotten through the first interview and was offered a second. Of course, this next interview would be in person, and I would have to employ a whole new level of skills to help her see beyond the hue of my skin.

As she handed me the water, I saw the muscles in her face give way to a faint smile as she remembered that she liked me. After all, that is why she called me in for a second interview. What had changed? She liked me sight unseen on the phone. Trying to relax, I continued warmly smiling, hoping to put her at ease with me. But her struggle continued, and she couldn't shake the fact that she liked me and concluded on the phone that I would be a good fit. If she denied it now, she would also have to admit that she was biased somehow—and of course, she was not.

I sat there quietly, in my navy-blue suit, with my hands folded in my lap while she evaluated me and my résumé. I was careful to wear a dainty pair of gold hoop earrings and a pair of one-and-a-half-inch black pumps, neutralizing my attire from her scrutiny. As she gave the paper her full attention, the silence was so loud I began to fidget, shifting my weight to the opposite side. I recrossed my legs at the ankles. And then, just as I shifted, she shifted too. I saw it happen.

Gradually her shrugged shoulders began to soften, and a faint smile began to dance around the corners of her mouth, easing her into a more relaxed conversation. The more we talked about where I'm from, my family, and then on to my career history and experience, the more she was reassured of what she already knew: she liked me. We traded stories and warm smiles, and she began to see me as an amiable person with dreams, goals, and a family that I love and want to help provide for. She saw me as a professional with attributes and valuable skills that would be helpful to have on her team. She saw me as the same person she imagined me to be on the phone.

She began explaining the company's values, benefits, and travel expectations, and it became clear that all reservations had left. The earlier surprise at my skin color had been erased and replaced by her surprise and delight at how much she wanted me to be a part of their team. "I would like to offer you a position," she said. "I would love to have you on our team." I broke out in a huge smile and enthusiastic nods of agreement, leaving no guesswork to my acceptance and appreciation.

"When can you start?" she asked.

"How about Monday," I replied, and the deal was done. We shook hands as I stood to leave, looking each other right in the eyes. Standing there in the moment, she saw me, and I saw her in full recognition and respect for each other.

As we stood to leave the conference room, I brushed my hands over the front of my skirt, and we headed toward the reception area, chatting and pausing along the way. She introduced me to other employees occupying cubicles and offices on the floor, making up the team. It was hard not to notice the absence of other people of color. Employees seemed to be surprised but genuinely happy to meet me. I've been here before—the only Black in my workplace. It is a part of my norm I have learned to accept. I welcome the opportunity to get to know people of the majority culture. But most of all, I look forward to them getting to know me and hopefully dispelling some of their apprehensions and preconceived notions about people of color generally and Black people in particular.[2]

When I got to my car, my prayers gave way to shouts of joy, "Thank You, Lord! Thank You, Lord!" praising God for what He

---

2 - The interview story is representative of multiple interviews throughout my professional career and is not intended to recount a specific person or company.

had done. First encounters at interviews are always a little dicey for me, never knowing how people will react, respond, or if they will even respect me. First days on a new job are equally tricky because the evaluation is always about more than my skills and experience. It's also about my professionalism and whether I will fit in with the team.

I realize that this is the same for everyone to a certain degree. But for people of color, the first day on the job takes on another level of complexity that is unseen and never voiced. I am expected to assimilate into a culture that was not made for me or with me in mind. I am expected to blend in and not cause any waves. I'm expected to make everyone feel comfortable with my presence and adjust when people become uneasy around me. It is up to me to keep my eye on everyone's attitude and whether they are growing perturbed or on edge. The tension is sometimes palpable, and uneasiness is commonplace. Once we move beyond the *getting to know you* phase and I am accepted as an ordinary person with ordinary aspirations, the anxiety diminishes. Then I can be myself or as close to myself as others are comfortable with.

I thank God that she was able to put her bias toward people who don't look like her aside and decide to move beyond the awkwardness of the situation. She trusted her instincts and what was staring her right in the face—a friendly, hardworking, and experienced person who would make a valuable contribution to the team.

That took courage on her part and on mine too. Every day we had to continue to prove to ourselves and others that she made the right decision to hire me. Every day for a long time, the subtle scrutiny continued, and I had to prove myself over and over again. The expectations were high—very high—arriving early, leaving late, doing my share and more until, one by one, they accepted me as an equal part of the team. Then, finally, I could lower my guard and relax into a rhythm that everyone else was accustomed to enjoying.

When we think about scenes like this playing out, it's easy to deny that this could happen to someone in real life. How does hearing this scene play out make you feel? Are there people of color in your workplace, department, or office? If so, write down each of their names. See each of them in your mind's eye. Think about the work environment and their experience in the workplace. What do you contribute positively or negatively to the current reality in your workplace? What changes or improvements can you make in your work environment to provide a more pleasant one for everyone? Maybe the concerns in your workplace are bigger than you alone can affect. If so, what measures can be taken, and whose attention can you bring it to?

> *Dear Lord,*
> *The fact that this type of thing happened and unfortunately can still happen today is disturbing. Thank You for making me sensitive to situations like this. Please move me from inaction to action. Help me to be part of the solution. Please show me how I can help move things forward to a more positive outcome for people who are marginalized. Please give me the courage and bravery it will take to stand in the gap for people whose voices are not valued as much as mine. Lord, we need Your help. Please help us! In Jesus' name, I pray. Amen.*

Reflection

Here is a friendly reminder that we are fellow travelers on a profound journey towards unity in Christ. Just like any long journey, our hearts need regular check-ups. I urge you to pause and examine your heart when encountering a challenging chapter. Don't ignore these discomforting feelings. Instead, confront them in the presence of God. Proceed with a transformed and healed heart that resembles the heart of Christ Jesus.

CHAPTER

12

WHAT'S OFFENSIVE?

"Together" was the fitting one-word theme of the Cru15 conference that we were attending in the summer of 2015. I was already weepy due to the sensitive matter of *our movement toward ethnic diversity* being discussed on center stage when my dear white brother in Christ asked me this tenderhearted question, "Will you tell me when someone offends you?" The moisture in my eyes that had been on the verge of spilling over became pools that dropped to my cheeks and rolled down my face and then onto my blouse. He explained that a lot of times, white people don't even know what's offensive to Black people.

My emotional eruption prohibited me from speaking for several seconds. Still, from my contorted face and a voice he didn't recognize, I managed to squeak out, "That would be exhausting."

He replied, "How many times a day would you say someone offends you?" My reply to that question came even slower, hampered by my emotional state. In his attempt to lessen my pain but still get the answer to his question, he offered, "Once a day?"

Jumping at the chance to give a short response, I produced the words "at least."

He was noticeably taken aback by my response. Clenching his jaws, he began to blink away the matching tears that had started to form in his eyes. Our exchange visibly shook his darling wife too, who was sitting next to him and across from me in the cafeteria booth. She reached over and patted my left hand with a damp napkin tucked underneath. And with a lump in her throat, she mouthed, "I'm so sorry." Wads of paper napkins were now littering the table, moist with my tears of pain and their tears of love and concern. I managed to offer my friend a compromise. "How about I tell you when *you* offend me?" He agreed that would be helpful.

We are both from Louisiana. Although there is just an hour or so distance between our hometowns, our paths did not find a reason to cross until God called me to serve Him at StoryRunners. I like to describe our friendship as "fast friends" because it didn't take long to find commonality and move into lively conversations about home, growing up, our love for God, our families, and our passion for the missionary work we were blessed to do together.

He genuinely wanted to know. He did not want to be the cause of anyone's pain, especially not mine. The sincere innocence of his question and desire to never be that person who unknowingly offends a person of color touched me deeply. His question also revealed the value he and his wife placed on our blossoming friendship and their strong desire to understand my experience—

my reality. They wanted to learn, which was the first big step in our diversity journey.

I knew their hearts and was inclined to push through my pain and emotions to continue the conversation. I pressed on to explain how it is for African Americans, especially in the South, where every day can dispense its own dose of offenses depending on whom you encounter.

Then I looked him squarely in the eye and said, "I choose not to be offended before the offense. Choosing to forgive is a way of life for most Black people. If you don't, you would not be able to move forward; you would just stay stuck and unable to get through life." I continued, "People were amazed by the incredible ability of the families of the victims in the church shooting in Charleston to forgive the shooter so quickly. Well, that's what we African Americans do—we have to. We forgive, dismiss it, and move on, or it will eat you up inside." So much about our lives has changed since this conversation in 2015; the most profound thing is that many of us work from home now. There are days I don't even leave my house, not even to go to the grocery store. Even with fewer in-person encounters, these incidents still happen occasionally and more often than one would probably think.

Like my friend, many people from the majority culture would readily admit that they are not even aware of what is offensive to African Americans. And how can you avoid or apologize for an offense if you don't know your words or actions are harmful? (We were obviously not talking about or overlooking when people are intentionally offensive.)

Allow me to take a moment and explain what I would regard as an offense, at least in the context of my friend's question. An offense is when someone does or says something offensive, and the recipient experiences the act or language negatively, ranging from unpleasant, impolite, distasteful, rude, insulting, or even nasty or downright hateful. Offenses are nuanced and can be further shaped by a person's tone, inflection, and expression. Toss any one of these adjectives at someone's feelings, emotions, and life experiences, and you are sure to harm someone in some way. It can play out in an interaction that brings on a distant memory that was particularly painful, uncomfortable, or sad to recall. Offenses can be soft and subtle or as bold as a slap in the face.

Sometimes, something said triggers a person's specific pain point. Choosing not to be offended is a way of managing that hurt and remaining positive. Forgive—forget it—and go on about your business is a common and necessary attitude in African American culture. Don't get stuck in a negative cycle! Some things you have to ignore and pretend they didn't happen. Others are acknowledged and quickly excused. But no matter how harmful or upsetting it is, it's still wise to let it go. Deciding to release it at once is in one's own best interest. Or better yet, it is the practice of choosing in advance not to be offended when someone says or does something that comes across as insensitive.

When I start to engage in a conversation like this one with my friend, I usually state early in the discussion that nothing you can say will offend me. I have already purposed in my heart not to be offended, so please speak freely—I know your heart. The optimism in me believes that most offenses that occur are unintentional. Personally, I don't go around looking to be offended or waiting for it to happen, but when it shows up, it stings all the same.

Whether the situation is an all-out affront, insult, or slur, or something that is a slight, a snub, or rubs you the wrong way, it is hurtful, upsetting, or disturbing. Whether intended to cause offense or not, as Christians, we must all exercise as much grace as we can to bring God glory and by our example.

One could say, "Well then, don't be so easily offended." I would say that, hopefully, no one is living life looking for offense any more than the offender is looking to offend—it just happens at the most unexpected time. It raises its head and takes a swipe at the heart of a person going about their day, and interrupts an otherwise joyful day.

Do you get past offense? Yes. The question is how fast or slow it takes the pain or embarrassment to subside. Does one offense put you on heightened alert for the next one? In my case, I would have to say sometimes. While unsure when it may come, due to my life experiences, I'm sure that it will. However, I consciously try to go on with my day and deal with my hurt before God instead of bracing for the next blow.

My sweet friend was asking that as we serve in ministry daily, and we go about doing life together, would I please tell him when I encounter something that is offensive. We remain friends some ten years later. They moved to Texas, some three hours from our home. And even though they live closer than before, it takes an effort to stay in touch, as most friendships do. So, a couple of times a year, we meet at a halfway point to catch up on ministry, family, and just getting older. We enjoy their company and they ours. I love their heart for ministry and Kingdom unity. And when we part, I'm reminded that it will not always be like this. When we get to heaven, we will enjoy eternity together in the presence of our Lord.

CHAPTER
13

WHERE I FIRST FOUND HOPE

"You don't really know the people you serve," I said frankly but lovingly to my passionate friend, who was trying to understand the plight of people in the neighborhood he serves. Week after week, I would drive to the Christ Evangelical Presbyterian Church (now Christ Presbyterian Church) to meet with three white brothers for a noon Bible study. We were months into the book study and had become comfortable and trusting of one another. We were friends, and we remain friends. Unpacking our lunches from home or the nearest sandwich shop on our drive into town, we would enter into small talk, checking on one another's families. The upstairs classroom didn't have much to offer in the way of distraction—the walls were bare, and the tables were in a U-shape, ensuring we connected equally and captured every gesture and expression of truth.

This particular day, we were deep into studying one of the secrets in Rabbi Daniel Lapin's book, *Business Secrets from the Bible*, and the subject turned to the inner-city concerns that puzzled my friend's mind. I proclaimed, "The kids need hope—the hope of a path out."

My dear Bible study friends inquired further with the eldest of the three asking me, "Where did you get your hope?"

I paused for a while, my eyes searching the corner of the ceiling for the answer to his question, intuitively knowing the answer but searching for the precise distinction that was elusively flitting in and out of my memory. I pilfered through my childhood memories and my childhood friends and foes, looking for the subtle difference that brought about a distinct difference.

My mind went down memory lane in search of the source of my hope. It led me past my wonderful parents, as incredible as they were. My search led me past my loving extended family and even my solid church family, although they were critically important. I could attest that such would be true for many growing up in my environment in my day and age.

I finally spoke, after a long pause and the uninterrupted silence of my patient friends who were careful not to disturb my thought process. My mind settled on the wooden benches that teetered up and down on the uneven floorboards of the First Baptist Church in the quarters. The little white church perched on the corner was the center of the community, and at one time it also served as the schoolhouse for the colored kids. A narrow kitchen spanned the length of the church in the rear, doubling as classrooms that separated the big kids from the little ones.

To my surprise my answer seemed too simple, so I pressed on, silently asking myself, "Where did this hope originate? Where did I get this hope?" I got drawn into even deeper thoughts as I continued to rummage through sweet and savory memories of my childhood. Without warning, I began to feel hot tears pool on the brim of my bottom eyelids and then race down my cheeks, one after another.

I could finally put my finger on what I believe made all the difference, and I do mean *all* the difference. "It was Bible stories! Yes, that was it, the Bible stories. I grew up hearing stories of the Bible like David and Goliath, Daniel in the lions' den, the three Hebrew boys, and Joseph's story with his coat of many colors. The one thing all of these stories had in common was hope and the fact that God always came through and helped the underdog." The underdog always won and achieved great things with God's help. For the first time, it dawned on me that the hopefulness of their stories gave me hope and a belief system that told me all things are possible with God.

It became a part of my psyche to expect good things to happen, no matter how bad the situation seemed. God always came through for those who were faithful to Him. These stories embodied "And we know that in all things God works for the good of those who love him, who have been called according to his purpose" (Romans 8:28, NIV).

This discovery was monumental because before now, try as I may, I was unable to trace my experience back to this differentiator, and there it was. For the first time, I was able to attribute the difference maker as *hope*—hope and expectation for a bright future. Many children grow up in nice homes with great parents who love them, so I was sure that wasn't it, even though it was a contributing factor. The *hope factor* etched in my mind a pathway that led to bigger and better things, endless possibilities, and dream upon dream.

As I pen this, I am inspired by the awareness that each of the Bible heroes I've mentioned eventually ended up in a palace, serving God. Unlike the storybook endings of childhood tales we are told, Bible stories are true and have the power to change lives. I am convinced that my life differed because of these inspiring biblical accounts of young people following God and the hope that following God brings.

What an aha moment! These stories, so perfectly narrated with a supporting flannel board, created mental imagery that seeped into my subconscious mind and cast a vision of the impossible being the norm for children who put their trust in God. They were the springboard for my expectations in life. "That's where my hope came from," I proclaimed. He was as astonished as I was at my discovery and my confident answer. The best news is that this great hope was and is free!

I no longer push back when someone says, "You're different." I gladly attribute that difference to the Word of God taught to me from an early age. Continuing to study God's Word, I am forever changing, and yes, I am different for His glory.

Later, as I continue to reflect, I think about the young and tender minds of children growing up in less than pleasant circumstances, hearing and seeing things that dampen the spirit and douse hope, robbing them of their dreams. I allow my mind to picture images, some of which I have only seen on television but I know to be some kid's reality. I don't shy away from the bleak future of that little child if something miraculous doesn't happen or if someone inspired to care doesn't intervene.

By this time my friend and I were in a heavy, candid conversation in a genuine attempt to get to the root of the answer and, therefore, maybe, just maybe, a real solution. My friend was asking me, "What was the difference-maker?" This generous friend of mine has been an advocate for underprivileged kids for many years. He has tried hard to understand and offer solutions to break the cycles of poverty and pain in young children's lives.

Black kids born in America are mostly born into poverty and some into abject poverty. Some are raised in cities, while others grow up in rural pockets of the country, on the other side of the railroad tracks, and down dirt roads with no outlets. Some are raised by farmers and laborers, and others by professionals and preachers. Some are born to loving parents and doting grandparents, while others are not as fortunate. Some have a father in the home, while many don't. I've seen children of all types coming from all kinds of situations, from all sorts of backgrounds, be "different," if I can use the term, and make a difference.

This time the "you're different" category I had so often been boxed into was begging for an answer. *What's different about you?* Before, when this label was applied to me, I would push back verbally. I would say, "I'm not different; my whole family is just like me. Furthermore, I have a whole host of extended family and church family members that are also like me." For years this was my response to this observation by others. Little did I know that this accurate statement gave me profound insight into the truth that went unnoticed before, maybe because while I was being flattered, I took no pride in being called "different." Here I was searching, searching, searching my mind for the shred of difference that must have been evident to produce a different outcome.

Living in this great country (the United States), we have many opportunities, but we don't have the same opportunities. We don't start at the same place; we are not all afforded the same amount of resources; including but not limited to inspiration, outlook, parental and family support, and access to the best teachers and schools. No, I beg to differ with anyone who says, "We all have the same opportunity." Yes, I do believe we all have the opportunity to better ourselves, but even then, the opportunities to do so will differ based on access to the things I've already mentioned and more.

If you are still having trouble embracing this idea, examine your own life and think about the kids in your school who were smarter than you and had more than you. Maybe their parents had more income than your parents, or they lived in a bigger house or went on summer vacations while you spent your summer days at the community pool.

Each experience, whether pleasant or unpleasant, impacts and shapes the life, the mind, and the future hopes of an individual. Again, I'm not saying we can't all improve our situation, but I am saying we are not all having the same experience. And that truth alone will deliver varying results and outcomes. I get it; you don't like excuses. God knows I don't either, and I'm not asking you to accept this as an excuse, but to please accept it as reality.

Your reality is different from the reality of others, as was mine, and countless circumstances affect how things played out, many of which neither you nor I had any control over. Again, I'm not saying we don't all have opportunities; I'm just saying, "We don't all have *the same* opportunities."

I hope this awareness is helpful and will cause our hearts to be a little more sensitive to the plight of others who are having a different experience from our own. Even if you are not inclined to extend a hand, an acknowledgment that we are not the same and therefore we cannot be experiencing the same things in the same way goes a long way in understanding the issues we face in our country. Put another way, we are all different, and therefore, we indeed have different experiences.

Before moving on, please take some time to reflect on your childhood and examine the various people in your neighborhood and the surrounding communities in this new light. How did you see people who were different from you back then, and how did you see yourself? Consider your own family, how many children there were, and the order of the sibling chain. Please take note of the difference in the age and maturity of your parents and maybe the difference in resources available over the course of time when they were raising children. Perhaps it afforded one child the opportunity of college but not the other. Maybe better clothes, better care, a bigger house, better vacations, or even better colleges and universities were available. Every variable can be a difference-maker.

I know you have heard the saying, "It's not what you know; it's who you know." Well, who did your parents know or not know that could have opened a door for you to a university or even a job? Whom do you know that you can just pick up the phone and ask for a favor for your child? What resources do you have access to that provide bigger and better opportunities for your children? All of these things change the outcome of a person's future and their future hopes.

Now think about that child whose parents may not have had the education or employment opportunities you have been afforded. Do you think that child will have the same opportunities as your child? Now play that scenario forward two or three generations as it relates to your future and the future of your children. Think about how this may have an impact on generational wealth or generational poverty. I'm just asking you to think about this and allow God to soften your heart in this area. Maybe, just maybe, you will have a change of heart and be able to empathize with others who are different and are having a different experience than you are having.

I know I've said this before, but it bears repeating: God made us different and placed us in different times in history, different geographical locations, and different socio-economic situations. We are different, but that doesn't mean our differences should divide us or cause us to treat one another differently. We are all part of the human race, and there is only one human race. We are all deeply loved by our Creator unconditionally. I hope and pray that we can learn to love one another unconditionally. I know that is our Lord's prayer too. Jesus prays to God the Father for all believers in John 17:20–23:

> *I do not ask for these only, but also for those who will believe in me through their word, that they may all be one, just as you, Father, are in me, and I in you, that they also may be in us, so that the world may believe that you have sent me. The glory that you have given me I have given to them, that they may be one even as we are one, I in them and you in me, that they may become perfectly one, so that the world may know that you sent me and loved them even as you loved me.*

CHAPTER
14

BE A GERRI

I pulled into the secluded country club after a forty-five-minute drive from my side of town. I donned my hooded cape as I got out of my car and broke into a long stride to get out of the cold, damp morning air. Traversing the lengthy hallways of plush carpet got my blood flowing and warmed me up by the time I reached the circular, floor-to-ceiling windowed banquet room. It overlooked a pond adorned with a waterfall. A foursome was approaching the tee box just on the other side of the pond.

"Thank you for always welcoming me so warmly," I whispered in Gerri's ear as she embraced me that chilly spring morning. The puzzled look on her face told me my comment required further explanation, so I continued. "Well, let's just say, not everyone receives me as warmly as you do." When her face went from confused to sad, I could tell that she got my meaning that time. With sadness in her eyes and moisture in mine, I explained further. "Gerri, when you wrap your arms around me so warmly, you validate me to the rest of the room, and others are more accepting and welcoming."

Her face continued to alternate between confusion and sadness and then changed to disgust. So I reassured her that I was so thankful for her, and she brightened again. I scurried on to mingle with the onlookers and witnesses of the embrace. Each of them flashed me a smile, extended me their hand, and invited me into their conversation. Unfortunately, there is not always a Gerri to greet me.

It's hard to believe that even in these modern times, I would need someone to vouch for me, but just because we are wearing the latest styles doesn't mean our thinking has kept up with our wardrobes. There are times when I have to ignore the faces that display disgust or wonderment at my presence. Searching for a welcoming smile, I cautiously gravitate toward the warmth that melts away the chill I sometimes experience. This scene plays out in a matter of seconds, and then everyone goes back to mixing and mingling.

Getting comfortable with my surroundings, I wait as the acceptance level normalizes somewhere around "tolerance" and "it's OK that she's here." Sometimes I even experience an "I'm so glad you're here." The room is always filled with a mixed bag of people's feelings about themselves and others. I remind myself that I am not responsible for how they feel about me or how they treat me; what I am responsible for is how I treat them and how I handle their treatment of me.

The next step is to slip into metamorphosis mode, where I begin to change from the insect in the cocoon that is easy to overlook into a graceful creature that is easy to be around and even welcomed to hang around. Unconsciously, I begin the delicate dance of making others comfortable with my presence. And just like that brightly colored butterfly that you can't miss against the green tapestry of nature, it is apparent that I am the only one of my kind in the room, no longer being tolerated but wooed into conversations.

Soon people begin to settle in and adjust to my presence. Then the new normal is that I'm the only Black person there. That's the level of acceptance with which I have to be comfortable. I could expect more, I could demand more, but that would make everyone even more uncomfortable. And how would that advance the change of acceptance that needs to take place? Just look at social media, and you can see how far we have to go in our acceptance of one another. The fact is, we need to retake some of the ground we had already gained.

In all of my life, I never thought we would be revisiting race relations like we are now facing in our day and age. I never thought my Black experience would need dredging up to shed light and hopefully bring solutions to the problem. But more stories like mine are not the only stories needed. More examples like Gerri's are needed to break down color lines by simply extending hugs, friendly introductions, and bi-racial friendship exhibited for skeptical onlookers to see. Then skepticism will give way to acceptance, and right on its heels will be inclusion. It's incredible how fast the heart can shift through this chasm of color barriers. It's amazing to see and much more amazing to experience.

I wish more people were like my *color-full* friends, who embrace people of all colors. Sadly, they are somewhat rare in all ethnicities. This rareness is not because there are not others like them (because I believe there are), but because many people lack the courage to stand up for others who are different. In the fallen human state, people are more interested in protecting their self-image than in taking the chance of being ridiculed or shunned by their peers.

Standing up for others demands courage and is a risky business. I would not ask any of my friends to take this stand for me, so I am always pleasantly surprised when they do.

Currently, hatred is spilling out from the recesses of people's minds into the light of day. I hope that those who carry the banner of love, especially in Jesus' name, will have the courage to drown out the voices emboldened by hate, and smother the smoldering coals that are just waiting for a breath of oxygen to fan them into flames.

Follow the lead of my dear friends, who are extraordinary in the art of breaking the color barrier. Now that I think about it, it's probably not an art at all; it's just who they are. I thank God for these friends because they save me from these intensely uncomfortable moments all the time. Christian brothers and sisters, we have the answer! Let's take Jesus' never-ending love to a world that desperately needs it.

Love is patient and kind; love does not envy or boast; it is not arrogant or rude.

It does not insist on its own way; it is not irritable or resentful;

it does not rejoice at wrongdoing, but rejoices with the truth.

Love bears all things, believes all things, hopes all things, endures all things.

Love never ends.

(1 Cor. 13:4–8)

Reflection

Are you speeding alone, ignoring the "check heart" light that is flashing?

In your eagerness to get to the end, are you driving past areas that need repair? Remember, you are not alone on this journey. The Lord is with you, ready to examine your heart and fix what needs repair. Neglecting an issue often results in significant consequences in the future. Wouldn't pulling in for a private heart check with God be wise? Allow the Lord to identify the source of the problem, and with your permission, fix it for His sake and glory.

_____

_____

_____

_____

_____

_____

_____

_____

_____

_____

_____

_____

_____

CHAPTER

15

FIRST CHOICE

The waitress showed us to one of the last tables available among the hungry lunch crowd. This Mexican restaurant, with its colorful décor, was a lunch hot-spot that would become a repeat when I visited the home office of the ministry where I served. After the four of us took our seats, we perused our menus to the constant humming of chatter accented by the clanging of silverware hitting the Mexican stoneware that held the most delicious piping hot entrees. Catherine elevated her voice to continue the conversation we had been having as we waited to be seated. She expressed, "You were my first choice on the phone interview, and you were my first choice at the interviews in Houston."

I smiled at her from across the table and returned with a quick, "I couldn't tell; you never let on that I was your first choice."

I had answered a pop-up advertisement one Monday morning while listening in on a weekly call and sorting through my emails from over the weekend. *Church Development Representative*, the job ad read with the description and salary, which was more than I had ever made. Before I finished reading the description, I dialed the phone number provided, which surprised me because, before that moment, I had never considered applying for a "Christian" job. I had spent twenty years in the travel industry, and although I was actively serving at my church, employment at my church had never been something I had seriously considered.

"How well do you know Houston?" the voice on the other end of the phone asked.

Without hesitation, I responded, "Like the back of my hand," which was no exaggeration. The ability to understand maps and directions is one of the God-given attributes I possessed long before navigation systems were all the rage.

"Have you ever worked in ministry?"

"No—well, let's just say I've never been paid to work in ministry." I had found many ways to volunteer and serve over the years.

That day I gathered all of my volunteer experience and slapped it at the bottom of my résumé:

- Serving in children's ministry–Sunday school teacher to twenty kindergarten students.

- Formally held the position of evangelism ministry campus coordinator, 2004–2011.

- Led a team of fifteen volunteers in starting an annual golf classic, which has provided numerous educational scholarships for the past fifteen years and continues to grow in proceeds and the number of scholarships granted.

- Recruited and directed a team of more than forty volunteers in launching the first annual TCWW Angel Tree Christmas program and party for more than seventy children of incarcerated parents, which included the raising of funds, gifts, and volunteers.

- Founded Eternal Gift Givers in 2005, an evangelism ministry that helps empower Christians with an evangelistic tool (audio CD) to share the gospel of Jesus Christ.

At 10:10 PM that night, I emailed my résumé to Faith Comes By Hearing with an earnest prayer that I would get this job.

The following morning, I was on my patio enjoying my quiet time with the Lord, and while I was wrapping up my time, I decided to read just one more devotional. So I picked up a devotional book by Joyce Meyer, *Starting Your Day Right.* The last sentence of the devotion said, "Throughout the day today, occasionally stop what you are doing and ask Him [God] if there is anything He wants to say to you." So I thought to myself, *OK, I'll do that sometime.* And I heard in my spirit, *Do it right now.* So I say out loud, "OK, I'll do it right now." I then bowed my head with my hands turned palms up and quieted my spirit, and said, "Lord, is there anything You would like to say to me today?"

Immediately, I heard in my spirit, "The position is yours." Of course, this response to my question was not at all what I expected. This was the first time I ever had a conversation with God like this: I ask a question, and He answers.

I began to silently question myself, *Who said that? Did I say that? No, if I had said that, I would have said, "The position is mine." Was I thinking about that before I prayed? No, I wasn't thinking about that.* After a thorough examination of my thoughts and frame of mind, I concluded that I had indeed just heard from the Lord.

A couple of days later, I received a call to set up a phone interview. All I knew to do to prepare was pray, and pray I did. When the time came for the phone interview, I grabbed my prayer shawl, went into my home office, draped my shawl over my head, and continued to pray until the phone rang. I never removed the shawl for the duration of the interview. A couple of days later, I received a call for an in-person interview. The human resources director would fly into Houston from Albuquerque, New Mexico, to interview a couple of other applicants and me. I was instructed to be prepared to do a presentation on Faith Comes By Hearing ministry. "Do you want me to do a PowerPoint presentation or just a presentation?" I asked. She said, "You can do whatever you would like." She gave me several options for interview dates, and I agreed on Friday, August 8, 2008.

I was suspicious when she asked me if I would like to go to lunch with Catherine Jackson after my interview. This was a first. I had never had anyone ask me before the interview even took place to go to lunch with the interviewer after the interview. Was this a setup to see how I would handle myself? Maybe to check out my table manners? Sure it was, but that was no problem; I would just have to be on my Ps and Qs.

The interview that Friday morning went well, and the lovely, soft-spoken Catherine Jackson was professional, strong, and competent in her approach. She never let her guard down or showed any revealing clues as to her approval of me from start to finish. We got along well, but she never tipped her hand or gave me any indication that she preferred me over the other candidates, whom she had interviewed earlier in the week. I left feeling pretty good about the interview but didn't know how she felt.

"Where would you like to eat?" Catherine asked.

"Oh, it doesn't matter," I replied.

"How about Joe's Crab Shack?" she offered. It was then that I realized this was not a test of my table manners. After all, how do you assess one's etiquette while eating crab and such things? So I relaxed a little and ordered something manageable to eat without the messiness of crustaceans. After lunch, we said our goodbyes and went our separate ways with only an "It was nice meeting you, and I'll be getting back with you soon" between us. The weekend crawled on into the next week, and I remember thinking several times, *When is God going to tell them the position is mine?*

The call finally came in, inviting me to fly out to Albuquerque to visit the ministry headquarters of Faith Comes By Hearing. I would be staying at the founder's home on Thursday night and then tour the ministry and interview that Friday morning. The cool misty morning began with a hot pancake breakfast at a large natural wood table lined with fruit and condiments. Jerry and Annette Jackson were accustomed to having people from all over the world in their home, which doubled as a hospitality house/ retreat for people coming to visit the ministry. It was simple but comfortable, and the Jacksons knew how to make someone feel right at home with their warm conversations balanced with respect for privacy.

Every chance I got, I called my husband who was home praying to report what was happening. Based on my previous experiences in seeking employment, this was a strange arrangement for an interview process. But I went with it, knowing that God had already decided my future with this ministry and, therefore, vetted them in the process. I felt safe and cared for by the Jacksons.

The three of us headed into the office just after the last of the breakfast dishes were put away. Annette insisted that I ride up front with Jerry, and before we could enter the on-ramp to the major freeway, Jerry requested, "Tell me your story." I had already told him about our blended family. Our children were young adults now, but when we married, they were five, nine, and ten. I had shared some of my dreams and aspirations over breakfast, so I picked up my story when I began teaching vacation Bible school as a twelve-year-old. When I finally paused, Jerry asked if I would be willing to share my testimony at the morning staff meeting.

I agreed, not fully knowing what I was getting into. Within fifteen minutes of arriving at the office, there I was in front of the entire ministry family sharing my testimony, tears and all. As Jerry introduced me to the hundred or so "worker family" members, as they are affectionately called, his introduction started with apologizing to Catherine for getting things out of order, and not checking with her first about presenting me to the staff. With a big smile on her face, her response chuckled out, "It's OK." She affirmed that it was not a problem, and Jerry continued with his introduction. This was the first clue that I was her favorite candidate.

As they escorted me around from department to department of the sprawling warehouse office, I saw only one other person who looked like me, the now late Ray Warrior, language recording manager. But that didn't bother me in the least; this was my norm, being the only Black person or one of the few in corporate spaces. Later that day, after a battery of personality evaluations, aptitude tests, and more interviews with those I would report to, Catherine Jackson offered me the position of church development representative for Houston. I was so relieved and so excited I could hardly contain my smile and composure.

This position would be a significant pay increase for me. In fact, this was the only time in my work history (other than the nine months I was a flight attendant for Continental Airlines) that I was sure I would be compensated at the same rate of pay as my white counterparts. I was sure of this because the salary was posted with the position. On the flight back to Houston, I must have thanked

God for the entire plane ride home. This equitable salary would afford us more financial margin, options, and opportunities.

On my assessment of my previous jobs, there was no way that a white man, head of a household, raising a family was receiving the same compensation as me. There was practically no way a white woman living in the chic parts of the city was living on the same paycheck I brought home. How could they have been making it economically on what I was being paid? Yet there was no way ultimately to prove this at the time. Causing waves by asking those types of questions that can easily be denied could cost you your job, and then where would you and your family be with no job and no paycheck? Still, to this day, data indicates that most minority men and women make far less than their white counterparts in the same positions.

Imagine what decades of substandard pay does to a person's ability to provide the necessities for their family. It affects everything—what you eat, what you wear, what you drive, and where you live, which affects how you see yourself and how others see you. According to Pew Research[3], racially based income inequality has been a persistent problem for as long as this data has been collected.

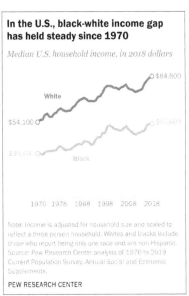

In the U.S., black-white income gap has held steady since 1970

Median U.S. household income, in 2018 dollars

$84,600

White

$54,100

$41,400

Black

1970 1978 1988 1998 2008 2018

Note: Income is adjusted for household size and scaled to reflect a three-person household. Whites and blacks include those who report being only one race and are non-Hispanic. Source: Pew Research Center analysis of 1970 to 2019 Current Population Survey, Annual Social and Economic Supplements.

PEW RESEARCH CENTER

---

3 - Chart copyright Pew Research. https://www.pewresearch.org/wp-content/uploads/2020/02/FT_20.02.04_EconomicInequality_3.png?w=620, accessed June 26, 2024.

The median incomes represented here reflect the national reality and disparity between these two races. By 2018 Blacks are just rising to the income levels that whites obtained back in 1970. Imagine making the same amount of money for the last forty-eight years while others' income continues to increase every year. And if that is not discouraging enough, imagine you were not even making the same amount to begin with. Imagine being stuck at your 1970 sub-par income while the price of everything is going up. Imagine it taking almost fifty years to earn the income your white neighbors earned back in 1970.

How would it affect what you can afford and what opportunities you can give your children? What difference would it make when it came to where you live and where your children attend school, or if they go to college at all? How many more vacations would you take if you had another $33,000 a year for the last fifty years? This single factor naturally becomes a negative reality for people caught in the cycle of being underpaid for generations. The same is true in the most positive way for the white majority receiving higher wages that continue increasing and compounding year after year for generations.

I was so happy at Faith Comes By Hearing, serving first as a church development representative in Houston, connecting with the top one hundred churches in my beloved city. After about two years, I began visiting some of the top one hundred churches in the Dallas Metroplex, and afterward, I was assigned the task of calling and visiting the top one hundred churches in the United States. I crisscrossed the country, connecting with missions pastors at churches with a vital mission focus.

Later, I was asked to handle major donor relationships in the interim while they found someone for the role. This was God's gracious way of easing me into a full-fledged fundraising role. I used to say, "They don't know it, but I would do this for free." I continued in this role until it was as if God called my bluff, and surprisingly, I was let go.

God had always been faithful in showing me the writing on the wall before a job ended and even lined up my next assignment ahead of my exit date. This was not one of those times. This time was different; it was abrupt and unexpected. I was devastated and confused. I was looking for God everywhere and didn't understand what He was doing during this time.

Within a few days, God called me to serve Him at Cru. This new assignment required me to raise my own salary by soliciting donations so I could serve as a development representative with StoryRunners. After evaluating our family budget, my husband and I arrived at the amount needed to cover the balance of our needs. This would result in a significant pay cut.

After being commissioned as a missionary, followed by thirteen months of raising the funding needed to cover my salary, my faith in God was stronger than ever. God showed me His desire to have lots of people involved in supporting the work of completion of the Great Commission and bringing the gospel to unreached people groups using oral Bible stories. My journey and growth in fund development only grew, and my trust in God to provide for His Kingdom's work grew exponentially. God knew exactly what I needed to continue growing in my spiritual walk with Him.

After I had served six years at Cru, God gave me an opportunity with another ministry where I was not responsible for raising my salary. After months of vetting, interviews, and evaluations, they offered me the position. I went through the entire hiring process seeking only God's will for my life and whether He was calling me to this new position. I purposely did not inquire about the salary or benefits, because none of that mattered if God was calling me to serve Him at this new ministry. I didn't want salary and other perks or any pros or cons to influence my decision. I only wanted to hear from God and follow His will for my life.

When they broached the subject of salary expectations, I expressed that I was sure they were going to compensate me fairly for the role. We finally had a conversation about my salary, after I was sure God had said *yes,* this is where I would be serving Him next. In thirty-seven years of work, career, and ministry, this was the first time I had the boldness to address the inequalities I had experienced over the years. I tearfully shared about the decades I had been underpaid and denied the salaries of my white male and female co-workers who did the same job as me. I expressed that I would be hurt and disappointed if I discovered that I was not being compensated at the same rate of pay as my white counterparts.

I probably would not have had the courage to advocate for myself in this way had this topic not been frequently in the news recently and a large part of the national conversation in our country. Equal pay for women and people of color had taken center stage, exposing the inequalities imposed on people with little voice. The attitude that "you are lucky to be offered the job" is prevalent and debilitating, especially for a person of color, asserting themselves and haggling over the pay.

The fact that we were having a conversation at all was honoring. I also knew the leadership had my best interest at heart and sincerely desired to affirm me by doing what was right for me. I felt like God was finally redeeming me in this area, and although this would not make up for all the years of lesser pay, He was righting this wrong here and now. I knew at this moment that God was orchestrating my move to this new role and giving me the boldness to speak up. I felt genuinely loved that day and extremely grateful to God for this new assignment.

Dear Lord,

Thank you for using me in Your service, and regardless of the worth that man puts on me, You see my worth and consistently meet my needs. Thank You for always providing for my family and me. You have always been faithful in Your provisions. It should not take laws to make people treat one another fairly. It should not take the assertion and insistence of people demanding equal treatment if everyone simply treats others the way we want to be treated. Lord, please stir the hearts of those in charge who can right this wrong and do the right thing. Father God, I trust You to make this right in Your timing and according to Your will. In Jesus' name. Amen.

CHAPTER

16

GRAY GIRL

Nothing could have prepared me for what came out of this pastor's mouth. "Oh, so you're a gray girl," he said from across the desk. I had barely gotten myself situated in the chair before the insult came hurling directly at me. At first, I didn't know what to make of it; after all, no one had ever called me a *gray girl* before. I had never even heard the term until that very moment. My mind began to clumsily connect the dots, not black, not white, and then like someone had pushed me from behind, my thoughts stumbled into—*Black plus white equals gray*. My mind sputtered as if trying to make sense of a bad joke, only it was not a joke—he was serious.

I had heard terms like *mulatto* to describe light-complexioned Black people (which I am not), but "gray girl"—that was a new one for me. When it dawned on me what his derogatory statement implied, it took everything I had in me to keep my composure. I don't remember what I said next, as I sized up the clever-as-a-fox smirk the African American pastor had on his face. I determined I would not be shaken by his sly comment. No, I would do what I came to do regardless of his biased opinion of me. I took the below-the-belt gut punch he had just landed, but I would not give him the satisfaction of knowing the intensity of the body blow he had just dealt me.

As a sign of protest, I sat up straighter than before, and like in the childhood game Simon Says, I took one giant step forward over his uncouth comment, swallowed my flushed feeling, and started into my introduction of the ministry I was there to represent. It was a good thing I had delivered the presentation numerous times before and knew the information by heart, because time after time I had to will myself to take giant mental steps forward to complete the task and get out of there. I would have plenty of time to process this graceless display later—in private. I got through the presentation, sharing the mission and vision of the ministry to make God's Word available to nonliterate people groups in the form of an audio Bible in their language.

The real irony of it all was that I was there to discuss getting audio Bibles in different languages to unreached people groups around the world, and this pastor was confronting me with the authenticity of my ethnicity. For the love of God, I could not understand who I was talking to across the desk from me. At my age, I thought I had experienced every kind of insult from insensitive people. I always seem to be naively caught off guard when it comes from my own people.

As he escorted me through the dingy hallway back to the reception area, he couldn't keep his unbridled tongue from further insults. "When I talked to you on the phone, I thought to myself, *What does this white woman want with me?*" he admitted. There it was: he thought the woman he had scheduled the appointment with just a week ago was a white woman! I suppose he was unable to conceal what he initially thought of me. The shock that I wasn't a white woman dominated his thoughts until I walked out the door.

I wondered whether he had heard anything I said. Was he remorseful or ashamed for what he said or how it made me feel? Did he even care? Apparently, this encounter left an indelible impression on me, as it has made its way into this conversation. We cannot honestly know the amount of pain we inflict on another person. We can only understand the depth of hurt we experience when we are in pain. I shudder to think of causing someone pain in this and other ways, but I cringe because I know I have.

I don't think this pastor intended to injure me at the heart level that day, but he did. He probably wouldn't even recognize this encounter to be about him if he were to read this. I suppose that is how the fallen human spirit relates to life, living life from the inside out, never turning the table to see it from another person's perspective. I believe, until we can do just that, we will continue to hurt one another in unspeakable ways and have no regard for the injured. We will keep going around the proverbial mountain and never reach our promised land. God, please help us recognize our prejudices and place them at the foot of the cross.

If I had a dollar for every time someone has said, "You're different," well, let's just say that I would be in a different tax bracket. Being different or perceived as different can be a blessing and a curse. In an effort to fit into the American culture, work within corporate America, and obtain the American dream, I've had to polish up my speech, dress the part, and mind my manners. "You're different" can be stated as a compliment or be meant as an insult. And there is no mistaking which one is in use when I hear the familiar comment. My life has been riddled with comments of all sorts—some meant to cause harm, some meant to compliment.

The most confusing is when comments come from someone of color. During my childhood, a few knuckleheaded kids repeatedly accused me of "thinking I was white." Because I used proper English and enunciated my words, they thought I thought I was white. Well, not really; it was just their way of expressing their displeasure and discomfort with my proper speech. "How do you know what I'm thinking?" I would scoff back. "If you knew what I was thinking, you would know that's not what I'm thinking."

I cannot ever remember, not even once, wishing I was white. I've always been proud of being Black and representing my family and my race to the best of my ability. For that reason I was ridiculed throughout my childhood for my desire to be my best. I guess somehow, it made some feel uncomfortable. As a young girl, I wanted the taunting to stop, but I had to decide if I was going to be pressured into saying "dis and dat" instead of "this and that" when I spoke. The truth is, saying "dis and dat" was more uncomfortable for me than the taunting.

Second only to God Himself opening doors for me, speaking correct English has been the thing that has gotten me in the door more than any other single thing. Little did I know the thing I took so much flak for as a child was what made me more marketable in corporate America. As an airline pilot inquired, while engaging me on a trip when I was a flight attendant for Continental Airlines, "Where are you from?"

"Louisiana," I replied, enunciating every syllable.

"Well," he commented with a look of amazement as he closed the cockpit door, "you are a great ambassador for Louisiana." I took his generous compliment and went on happily serving the passengers in the first-class cabin. I think saying "Louis-i-ana" has less to do with pronunciation and more to do with the fact that my middle name is Louise.

~

Is being the first Black *anything* a blessing or a curse? Being the first puts you in an environment to be or feel isolated by both cultures—isolation from the majority culture because there may not be genuine and total acceptance and potentially isolation from your own culture because now your experience is different from what most experience.

As an adult, I can look back on it, shake my head at the absurdity of it all, and wonder how I made it past all of the prejudices of all the people whose complexion was even slightly different from mine. These various shades of "gray" gave some people status and demeaned others. These hues of gray were so subtle yet lived out so loudly. How is it that skin color give people the right to carry such pride and grants so much prestige? None of us made ourselves, yet we take pride in our looks as if we did. Not one of us had anything to do with our ethnicity, but we act as if we did.

Because of the grace of God, we are who we are, each of us living out who God has created us to be.

Because of the grace of God, we enjoy the place in life He has assigned us.

Because of the grace of God, we each wear the flesh He saw fit to bestow on us.

Because of God's grace, we are not stricken with an affliction when we take pride in ourselves and shun another.

God created each of us in His image and judging from the diversity of the human race around the world, God amply expresses

His love for diversity. God said everything He made was good (Gen. 1:31). Imagine His sadness when we deem something He made as *not so good* or *not as good in our eyes*. When I am marginalized by someone's vain opinion of what is beautiful, I have but to run back to my Creator to validate the way He made me.

I imagine Him looking at me with the loving eyes that can only be expressed by the Master Creator that He alone is. I consciously devalue the opinions of others toward me and hold tightly to God's loving fondness for that which He created for His good pleasure. In the moment, His loving eyes reflecting back the image of myself cancels out every hurt I have endured, intentionally or unintentionally.

Even now, I think back on those whom I would have thought myself better than, and my thoughts of superiority and pride grieve me. Knowing that I was and still am capable of inflicting the same hurts on another person sends me into a state of remorse and repentance.

> *Dear Lord,*
>
> *I am so sorry for calling what You called good not as good as me. Please forgive me! I know now that coping with my hurt by singling out someone I could marginalize for my own sake was selfish pride. Oh Lord, please forgive me for those past sins. And even now, when I fall into the trap of self-edification, which is always at someone else's expense, I repent and am truly sorry.*
>
> *Unfortunately, I know I probably will find it necessary to repent of this trespass again and again as I grow out of my particular prejudices and mature in my journey to be more like Christ. Lord, thank You in advance for Your patience with me. I'm so grateful that Your mercy endures forever. May I never take that for granted. In Jesus' name. Amen.*

Reflection

Please search your heart and evaluate if this is a prayer you can pray in all sincerity right now. If yes, pray this prayer from your heart and receive God's grace and forgiveness. If not, please take time to deal with prejudices, pride, and biases that stand in opposition to God's Word and the teachings of Jesus. Bring each of these issues to Jesus and ask Him to help you deal with them and create in you new ways of thinking and a renewed mind where pride and prejudices are no longer present.

CHAPTER
17

I'M GOING
WITH YOU

"Where are you going?" "How long are you going to be?" "Call me when you get there." "Be careful." "I plead the blood of Jesus over you." My voice got louder and louder the closer he got to his car. Repeat. Repeat. Repeat. This is a recurring line of questioning and dialogue at my house when my son heads out the door. Yes, even at thirty-seven, he gets this drill, "Call me when you get home." "You made it home." "You didn't call me." The funny thing is now he does the same thing to me: "Call me when you get home."

It is not my nature to live in fear. In fact, I've been known to say in the face of fear, "Don't you see this host of angels all around me? God is protecting me." And I know this because He always has. I trust God to take care of me, yet I've been conditioned to be concerned regarding my son and police interaction.

Personally, I have never been afraid of the police; I know they are there to protect me. I also know myself. I haven't done anything wrong, and I'm not likely to intentionally do anything to antagonize a police officer. I am at their mercy. I wouldn't say I like getting a traffic ticket; no one does. I've always felt I could handle myself when encountering the police by giving the officer what he asked for when he asked for it. I have also felt this was true for my son. He could handle himself, and God would take care of him.

I'm sure white mothers of young adults have various conversations about safety with their children as they head out the door with the car keys, but is it with the same sense of fear and dread? Are they concerned about the safety of their young adult sons like mothers of Black sons? When do I get to *not worry* about him? When can my concerns be laid aside? When do I get a break from mothering my adult son, who towers over me at six feet three inches? When will it be safe for him to travel the roadways of this country or the streets of his city without apprehension?

At thirty-six, he received his law degree during the early stages of COVID-19, so there was no graduation ceremony or pomp and circumstance. After canceling all of our plans, flights, hotel reservations, and celebratory events, a trip back to Milwaukee was still necessary for Mario to move out of his apartment. It was just a few weeks after the killing of George Floyd under a law enforcement officer's knee. American cities from coast to coast were alive with protests against the horrific scene that played out over and over on every television news station. This unimaginable incident grabbed the attention from the COVID-19 headlines and the rising death counts from this novel coronavirus. People poured into the streets to voice their outrage at the unnecessary killing on a loop on every size screen and device.

There couldn't be a worse time to be on the road, with this novel virus running rampant and the unpredictability of police officers too frequently making headline news for shooting a Black male motorist on a routine traffic stop. How could I let my son travel twelve hundred miles there and twelve hundred miles back in the volatile state of the country? I was not about to sit at home and worry every minute of Mario's twenty-four-hundred-mile trip to and from Milwaukee. No, that would be torture—that would be agonizing.

After some vacillation and counting the financial cost to fly and possible physical risk of driving, I decided to go with him. "Mom, I will be fine," Mario tried to assure me.

"I know you will, but I still think I will come. It will be safer if I'm with you," I responded. "If police officers see you as a family man, they are less likely to mistreat you," I rationalized. But this would mean a week off from ministry. Sure, I had the vacation time, but I should not have to use my vacation time to increase my son's safety on the roadways of my own country, I mentally protested. This is ridiculous, I thought, but necessary for my peace of mind. It would not be healthy or productive for me to sit at home trying to work during the weeklong turnaround trip.

Yes, I was afraid of COVID, but I was more fearful of what could happen to my son at the hands of the wrong police officer. Even now, as I write this and recall this time, my emotions spill over, and tears run down my face. That is my reality as a mother with a Black son in America. That's my reality as a wife, even though I know my husband knows how to handle himself if he gets stopped by a police officer.

A little more than halfway to Milwaukee, I began privately scolding myself for worrying to the point that I felt I had to accompany Mario to Wisconsin. We were enjoying the ride and the open road after being cooped up in the house for several weeks. "Not again!" I was not prepared to hear the devastating news of yet another Black mother receiving the call that a police officer had killed her son, but sure enough, before we got to Milwaukee, I did, reinforcing my decision.

God knows I wish I could take a break from the worry and concern, but month in and month out, my fears are reconfirmed by the interruption of *breaking news* of another Black man shot by a police officer. I wish I could turn the channel. I wish we could turn the page. I wish I could rip all the pages out of this book. I wish I could stop it from happening. My hope is that it would just stop happening. I pray that it would stop happening. I plead the blood of Jesus over those I love!

I'm just one Black mother of one Black son. My five sisters have sons. One sister has one son, another has two sons, another has one son, and another has one son, all of whom are grown men—and then another has three young sons. And that's not to mention my two brothers' two sons; they carry the family name. My brothers and their wives have the same concerns. I love my nephews and worry about them. The thought of losing even one of them causes my heart to ache as it shatters into countless pieces. To lose one of them at the hands of a police officer would be utterly tragic and unrepairable.

I feel my sisters' concern, usually in the form of a prayer request when their sons travel or are just going about doing what they are free to do as they chase their dreams. "Pray for Bryan; he is heading back to school today," my sister adds on our *family faith* conference call. Another sister will text, "Pray for Jonathon to have traveling grace today as he heads back home." I text in response, "Praying right now," with the *praying hands* emoji. Hours later another text finally lights up my phone screen. "Family, I made it home; thanks for your prayers." Then my phone begins to make beeping music as everyone on the family text begins a chorus of praising God for traveling grace, free from accident or incident.

When I'm in my car going from here to there and back, I pray for the young man standing on the side of the road with the police car's blue flasher intermittently lighting up his face. "Lord, I pray that there will be no altercation and this young man will make it back home to his family today. Thank You, God, for this officer and the work he is doing to keep the roadways safe to travel and that he will be able to return safely to his family. Lord, please protect them in this situation and let there be no incident or accident. In the name of Jesus. Amen."

Are our sons experiencing the carefree life their white peers enjoy if they are constantly plagued with concerns about such things? Are we experiencing the same things on the roadways of America? Do white mothers cover their sons in prayer as they say goodbye and walk out the door? Do white Americans concern themselves with the possibility of a bad experience with law enforcement? I submit to you—we are traveling on the same paved roads, but we are not all having the same experience. What are we going to do about it?

After the violent attempt to halt Congress's certification of the 2020 presidential election, I heard one of our white congresswomen being interviewed, and she commented on experiencing fear for her life for the first time ever. She likened it to the Black experience and said now she somewhat understood what Black people experience and what it might feel like to live in fear all the time. "Imagine that" was all I could say, to not have to be concerned about whether I need to fear another person, or whether I will experience animosity from another human being. The intensity of fear and despair may vary depending on the decade or the century you were born. This fear may be intensified depending on the region of the country in which you live. After the storming of the

Capitol, January 6, 2021, I heard one of our white congresswomen being interviewed, and she commented on experiencing fear for her life for the first time ever.

I'm left wondering what that must be like to not to have to calculate what I say and to whom, where I go, and when. Who is for me and who is against me? It's hard to tell, and the constant discernment of it all can be exhausting. Weariness becomes a condition of this life for people who look like me. Living in a nation with color lines that favor some and put others at a disadvantage can feel hopeless and tiresome. I am tired of crying and weary of worrying. But I must remain hopeful.

I've resolved to trust God and to pray. When that little tormenting thought enters my mind, I suppress it with my faith in God to take care of me and my family. I have to decide not to let worry overtake me. I have to make an effort and console myself with God's promises that He will never leave or forsake me. I find comfort in knowing that God is our shield and protection. Gradually, I begin to feel calm in my soul, and the grip of worry releases in the face of God's reassuring promises to keep us safe in His loving arms.

Reflection

I realize these topics can be troublesome to think about. If so, I invite you to ask yourself and God, "Why?" "Lord, why do I feel this way?" Take the time to reflect and receive from God.

_____

_____

_____

_____

_____

_____

_____

_____

_____

_____

_____

_____

_____

_____

_____

_____

_____

_____

_____

CHAPTER

18

MY LIVED EXPERIENCE

Church bombings and church shootings! I was eleven days old, and my sister Jackie would have been one year old that infamous late-summer morning, September 15, 1963, when the horrible news of the 16th Street Baptist Church bombing began broadcasting images out of Birmingham, Alabama. My young parents were only twenty and twenty-four years old when a bomb was set off by white Klansmen, maiming many and killing four young girls. Innocent and dressed in their best Sunday-go-to-meeting attire, their little lives were snuffed out by hatred. Black and white churchgoers across the country would return home from service to the scene of bombed-out rubble and little dead bodies on gurneys that we are all too familiar with as a part of our troubled American history.

My little life began during the earlier part of "the second half of the twentieth century," a phrase Rev. Martin Luther King Jr. would use to describe the age he lived in, in his "I've Been to the Mountaintop" speech. He was only thirty-eight years old at the time of his death. The beginning of the second half of the twentieth century was a turbulent time in our country when some whites opposed Blacks trying to gain their civil rights. Some whites were willing to fight and even kill for their cause to keep things the same. Scenes of Black's faces bashed in by policemen's batons, Black people on the receiving end of things thrown at them, Black people blasted with firemen's water hoses and gnawed at by police dogs were splashed across black-and-white TV screens on a much too regular basis. This tug-of-war persisted and even escalated during much of my young life.

I was two months old when President John F. Kennedy was shot to death, and the nation went into mourning. Lyndon B. Johnson became president of the United States of America, and just months before my first birthday, President Johnson signed the Civil Rights Act into law, advancing the civil rights movement and giving hope to parents like mine and children like me. I was four years old, and my young life was just beginning when Martin Luther King Jr. was shot, ending his life due to the hate-filled opposition to Blacks being treated fairly.

Hopefully, by now, you, too, are reviewing your lifetime line in parallel with these and other iconic dates in American history. Everything happens within a context. Time, location, and culture are all significant factors that affect experiences for better or worse. We know this to be true as we study the Scriptures. It is essential to consider the Scripture passage context to extract the correct meaning and not go away with the wrong application. If this is true of the Truth—Scripture—how is context important to our understanding of diverse cultural and social divides in America?

Think about the stress imposed on people for no other reason than they are not white. Think about the constant strain on a live born in this country. Now ponder just how much determination it takes to make something of yourself—how much mocking and sneering a Black person endures just to survive the day, the week, the year, this life. Dr. King could not know that his words "I can't sit idly by" in the letter he wrote in solitary confinement from the Birmingham jail, while I was still being formed in my mother's womb, would catch up with me almost sixty years later and inspire me to finish what God called me to do in writing this book.

I have outlived Dr. King's life span by more than twenty years now, and I find it necessary to implore my white brothers and sisters to take this cause one step further than Dr. King's invitation to join us in the continued struggle for Black people to be recognized and treated equally as God's children. Our goal to become one in Christ with all of God's children should be the aspiration of God's people—the Christian church today. Can we become one in Christ without first loving one another in genuine, authentic Christlike love? Can we become one in Christ without treating one another as equals? Does one happen without the other?

The Alabama church bombing in 1963 and Charleston's AME church shooting in 2015 are the disgraceful events that flanked my life when I started writing this book, the latter calling me out of anonymous service and into the light but hopefully not into the fire. I wrote most of this book between the tragic events of the Charleston AME church shooting and the killing of George Floyd in 2020, which served as a wake-up call to most Americans with eyes and a heart to see the unfair treatment exacted on people of color. In the five years between the bombing and the killing, the racial climate in America heated up and changed in ways I had not seen in my lifetime.

When horrific events like bombings, shootings, and killings happen, they should urge us into talks that bring healing to our country. Even more so, such events should call the church—the body of Christ, the family of God—off their pews and into talks with one another that lead us into a right relationship with our brothers and sisters. One of love and harmony. One of compassion and humility. Relationships of unity and oneness in Christ.

You know how it works in a healthy family unit when there is disunity. You gather around the kitchen table, and you talk it out, and you don't get to leave until there is a resolution, and unity and peace are restored in the home. Brothers and sisters, how is it that we yearn to be in a right relationship with God, yet day-to-day we go about ignoring our relationship with one another and still call ourselves a family, the family of God?

From ten-days-old to sixty-years-old, yes, there have been ebbs and flows of harmony, but hostility seems to never completely go out of style. The strife is simply over everyone being treated with common decency. The Lord mandates that His children love our neighbors as ourselves. How long will the people of God allow enmity among us to go unchecked? How long will we allow hatred's hot breath to smother out love's symphony?

I have been affiliated with a couple of Christian ministries for years. Shortly after George Floyd was killed, the leaders of these ministries reached out to me with an observation and confession about their organization's lack of diversity. I was told by one that I was the only Black person in that organization, and the other was grieved because there were no people of color in leadership and she wanted to do something about that. Dear brothers and sisters, because of God's Word and the work He continues to do in each of His children, I believe there is still hope for us. But our desire to be one has to be stronger than our desire to be comfortable or right. Our desire to understand one another must overrule our desire to be heard. Our desire to defeat the devil and his evil tactics to keep us separated and at odds with one another must rise up and dominate over the discord he sows among us.

If not for Christians, what hope do we have in this land? What hope is there for our children? We dare not hand down an America to our children where people and even Christian brothers and sisters are afraid of one another. We dare not leave this America worse off than when we arrived here. We dare not look like the world in our actions and reactions to the despair and diminishing of our beloved American lifestyle. We deserve better; our children and grandchildren certainly deserve better. Brothers and sisters in Christ, let's decide to do better. We can do this in Christ Jesus!

> *Dear Lord,*
>
> *We are Your children and citizens of Your kingdom, but we are also in this world. Please help us be a people set apart from feelings of enmity and hostility. May our love for one another shine through and pierce the darkness that is prevalent in our country. Lord, it is easy to get caught up in the emotions of it all but help us remember that our role is to show the world the love of Jesus. Please help us be constantly mindful that, as Your children, we are all in Christ. In Jesus' name. Amen.*

Reflection

At this juncture, you might be feeling weary and fatigued from your inner work. However, it's crucial to remember that the purpose of this journey is far greater than you, your church, or your country. It's about making the world aware that God the Father sent His Son Jesus to save us. There is no greater cause or reason to persevere in our quest for perfect unity than the cause of Christ. Your personal commitment to this journey is vital to whosoever will believe in Him.

_____

_____

_____

_____

_____

_____

_____

_____

_____

_____

_____

_____

_____

_____

CHAPTER
19

MY PRIVILEGE

Let me be the first to acknowledge and give thanks to God for the privilege I have experienced and still enjoy in my life. Yes, even Black people can be privileged. Even though I was born Black, and lived on what some would call the wrong side of the tracks, to parents with no college degree and none to speak of myself, I still live a privileged life.

— I am first privileged to be born in the wealthiest country on the planet.

— I am privileged to be born during times of peace and void of homeland wars.

— I am blessed to have been born to Christian parents and grandparents.

— I was blessed to have two loving parents in my home.

— I was blessed to be introduced to and accepted Jesus at an early age.

— I am blessed to be the first Black to receive various specific opportunities.

— I was privileged to have been raised with a sense of hope and a healthy outlook on life.

— I am blessed to have been raised in the fear and admonition of the Lord.

— I am blessed to have been guided by the Word of God from childhood.

— I am privileged to be in a country where all children, even girls, get an education.

— I am blessed with the wisdom of God.

— I am blessed to have the wise counsel of great parents.

— I am blessed to have a wonderfully close immediate and extended family.

— I am blessed and very thankful for an amazing husband and three fantastic children.

What a privilege and a blessing it is to experience the love of God daily!

Every blessing and privilege gives me an advantage in the world. Every advantage gave me a head start in my quest and pursuit of the American dream. Every first afforded my parents gave me a head start out of poverty into privilege. Every time I was the only Black represented, countless others were excluded. Every time I could look around the room and count on one hand the number of people who looked like me was an indication of the opportunity it was to be the first, the privilege to be the only, or the honor to represent my community as one of the few people of color in specific spaces then and now.

No matter what our station is in life, every one of us in the United States of America can claim some measure of privilege compared to people in developing parts of the world. Consider war-torn countries, countries devastated by hurricanes or earthquakes every few years, and countries plagued with drought and famine. Think about areas of the world where education is not a given and certainly not to girls.

We have so much for which to be thankful. We have so much privilege that it is normal, but just because something is our normal does not make it any less a privilege. All of these blessings and privileges raise these questions in me: For what purpose? Why me? What is my response to my privilege? What is my responsibility? Do I keep running ahead with the mindset that I've got mine; you get yours? Do I conclude that if you don't have what I have, it's because you are not trying hard enough? Do I look down on others in haughtiness and judgment? Certainly, these are ways one can respond, but I have a feeling it will not earn us a heavenly reward.

What would be a better response? How could I extend the privilege afforded me to others less privileged? What can I do to lift somebody up or extend a hand? These are great questions, but it must first begin with recognizing that we are privileged, and our privilege has a purpose, and I can guarantee you it is not to look down on others and scoff at them because they are not as privileged.

Recognize that most of the privileges we enjoy, we had absolutely nothing to do with. It is purely the grace of God, where we were born, the time in history we were born into, the parents we were born to, the ethnicity we were born with, the socioeconomic class we were born into, none of which we can take credit for, nor

PRAISE FOR THE FIRST, THE ONLY, THE FEW

should we take pride in. By God's grace, we are where we are, and we started life where we did. Sure, someone started life in a more privileged situation than you did. And indeed, others started life in less privileged circumstances than you or I. Can we simply be honest with ourselves and, at the very least, recognize this to be true?

Truth is the first step in moving forward—the truth that we enjoy certain privileges. Whether we are willing to admit it or not, we enjoy privileges others do not have because of the geographic, economic, ethnic, and natural order of things like natural disasters or the human effect of events like war.

Please don't look away or slough this reality off as nothing. It is a big deal whether or not we are open to seeing it as such. Using all of your human efforts, how long would it take you to obtain and acquire all of the comforts and favor that your privilege, as a matter of course, affords you?

As human beings, our necessities in life beyond air to breathe are clean drinking water, two or three meals daily, and shelter over our heads—any shelter. Beyond these necessities, everything else is a luxury and a privilege. Can you see your privilege now that you have stripped life down to the bare essentials? Let's start here and begin to grant others grace and understanding. Let's start here and begin to extend a helping hand. Let's start here and seek to employ our privilege to help others gain a similar advantage.

Let's not allow our privilege to blind us to the needs of others or allow calluses to grow over our hearts. Let's not allow our privilege to see others as *those people* or to think higher of ourselves than we should. Let's not allow our privilege to look down on others made in the image of God. Let's not allow our God-given privilege to create a bubble around us that only allows certain people access to the exclusion of others—others who started life with less privilege. Let's give all thanks to God from whom all blessings flow. "For it is [God] who gives you power to get wealth" (Deut. 8:18). "[God] supplies seed to the sower" (2 Cor. 9:10, NIV).

Let's not look down on others because of the goodness God has shown us. Let's give credit where credit is due—to God. If it were not for God's grace and His providence, we could just as easily be less privileged. I cannot lay claim to any of the privileges I was born into any more than you can.

We are one race under God. Not by choice but by His design! Amazing! By no choice of our own, we come into this world to parents whom we do not choose, into an ethnicity also not of our choosing, into a socioeconomic status again not of our making. And yet we move out into the world cloaked in the design that God has indeed chosen for us. Have you ever wondered why you were born white? or Black? or Asian or Latino? If you are an American, have you ever wondered why you were born in the richest, freest nation in all of history? Have you ever asked yourself the question, "Why was I born into such an affluent or contritely poverty-stricken family or neighborhood?" I clearly had nothing to do with the good faith and home I was born into. This would prove to be as important to my story as the time I was born. It was God who designed this life for me.

What are you and I going to do with this privilege?

> *Lord God,*
>
> *Thank You for every privilege You have graciously given me. Not because I deserved it but because You are good. Whether my parents, my geographic location, or the gifts and talents You blessed me with—all are because of Your goodness toward me. Let me not boast or take pride in these privileges. Lord, please forgive me for every prideful thought and haughty look or attitude. You could have just as easily given me a different lot in life. Thank You for forgiving me. And*

thank You for Your divine providence concerning me and the eternal salvation You have graciously granted me. Help me live a life that is deserving of it, showing others mercy and granting people the same grace You have given me. Thank You, good, good God! In Jesus' name. Amen.

CHAPTER
20

THEY, THEM, THOSE

Phrases like "they always," "all of them," "those people," are thrown around in the most dismissive way when someone is trying to differentiate one ethnicity or group of people from their own. We are all divinely created with ethnic identities, so let's be clear: I'm not saying we are all the same, nor must we all act the same. Our negative view of differences, cultural or otherwise, is what usually prompts someone to start or finish a sentence with one of these pronouns and phrases.

It's talk we only use when we are among our own kind. It's the kind of conversation we only use when we are sure the ones surrounding us will understand and agree.

It's the white man's fault.
It's the Black man's fault.
They always.
Those people.

Statements with these phrases in them usually don't end with a positive comment. Yet we are generally looking for agreement and reinforcement. Then the pile-on typically occurs, with no pushback from anyone within earshot.

I often wonder why these blanket statements that color an entire people with a large and negative brush are not challenged. I suspect there are at least two possible reasons for our silence in these situations. One is our lack of courage to speak up on behalf of all the people in a particular group who do not deserve that negative reputation. Or it could be that we lack knowledge of or a relationship with anyone from that group of people to speak out on their behalf. Both deserve our attention, commitment, and dedication to negate painting an entire people with the same brush.

Speak up and speak out!

I realize it can be risky to speak up for people who are different from you. It takes courage to speak out against this kind of negative talk. It is easier to keep your mouth shut; I know this because I have been in this situation and didn't quash the conversation with a positive comment. And I'm sure all of us can identify with experiences that welcomed our insight and perspective in the discussion, but instead we chose self-preservation and demonstrated it by staying silent. How do we muster up the courage to speak up on behalf of another ethnicity being torn down by the words of people in our clan, our tribe, our ilk, our posse, and our clique— people who look and think like me?

Likewise, it is not popular to go around speaking kindly of people who are being blamed for something in the minds of our peers. But we must push back for the sake of those in this group who are blameless of the spoken behavior. People are worth defending whether it will cost us something or not. You probably will not rise to the top in popularity for doing so, but hopefully, it will make you feel better that you said something and didn't let this negative comment go unchecked.

Additionally, it takes a whole lot more courage to say something positive in someone's defense and wait to see who will agree with you than it does to say something negative. I realize making bold, sweeping negative statements comes much easier than saying something considerate or edifying; it's because of our sinful nature.

Let me be the first to confess to God and apologize for the many instances when I have heard negative talk about a different ethnic group and either kept silent or agreed with the comment. Furthermore, I also need to confess those times when I was the one making the negative comment that started with *they* or *those*. I am genuinely sorry, and I'll check myself against this kind of demeaning talk about people different from me.

Confession is good for the soul. I submit to you, brothers and sisters, that what we need is a wholehearted confession. True confession admits that you are wrong, asks God to forgive that wrong, and fully intends not to commit that sin again. When we genuinely confess, God is faithful to forgive us for our sins (1 John 1:9). Our sins (once forgiven) are removed as far as the east is from the west (Ps. 103:12). And God no longer remembers our sins (Heb. 8:12).

That's the kind of forgiveness I need when I think of the thoughts I've had, the offenses I've harbored, and the things I've said that were less than kind. I do indeed feel like a filthy rag in the eyesight of God (Isa. 64:6). "None is righteous, no, not one," the Word proclaims (Rom. 3:10). We must all reckon with our disobedience and our sins of omission.

I know this will be hard because sometimes things happen, and we just want to vent with people like us and who identify with us. But I can assure you will experience a more incredible feeling when you speak up against the denigration of an entire group of people. Brothers and sisters in Christ, it will be challenging, but will you make every attempt to stand with me in this effort to change this about ourselves? I submit to you that there is a notable difference between *a sin* and a *sinful lifestyle*. The first is a one-time or rare offense, while the second is an ongoing, habitual, repeated offense without remorse, correction, confession, or renewing of the mind in this area. It is only natural that the unchecked sin will be repeated and become a part of a sinful lifestyle. So, how do we go about fixing it and making this right? It has to start at the heart level, a genuine personal change of heart.

Therefore, as God's chosen people, holy and dearly loved, clothe yourselves with compassion, kindness, humility, gentleness and patience. Bear with each other and forgive one another if any of you has a grievance against someone. Forgive as the Lord forgave you. And over all these virtues put on love, which binds them all together in perfect unity.

(Colossians 3:12-14, NIV)

We must first desire change; then we must pursue it with everything in our being. Like any habit we've tried to break, we must stay at it, failing sometimes and winning others. We must admit the wrong in our thought life and our perception of entire groups of people and be truly honest with ourselves and God about how we feel about people from different ethnicities and cultures.

We must ask ourselves the tough questions: Why do I feel this way? When did I start thinking this way? What have I done to prolong this type of thinking? How have I facilitated this type of wrong thinking? How have I promoted this type of erroneous thinking? How have I been a part of the marginalization of others?

We must be sincerely sorry for looking down our noses at another human being with high-minded thoughts. After all, they did not make themselves, and likewise, I did not make myself. The same God who made me made all. "Yet you, Lord, are our Father. We are the clay, you are the potter; we are all the work of your hand." (Isa. 64:8, NIV) Are we so daring as to tell God that someone He made is not good?

We are not all the same; even within ethnicities, we are not all the same. We are very different. Variety in ethnicities reveals the vast diversity in our God. These differences reveal the creativity and love God has for each of us individually. Ethnic diversity expresses the endlessly creative mind of our infinite God. We are all uniquely and wonderfully made for God's glory and to His credit.

> *Dear Lord,*
>
> *You have made each of us for Your own pleasure. Thank You that we are not all the same. May we see each individual person as valuable and made by You. May we experience the approval You expressed when You blessed humanity back in Genesis. Lord, please help Your people see diversity as a gift and individuality as a blessing from Your creative mind and hand. Help us not to scoff at our differences but revel in our diversity just as we delight in You, oh Lord. Amen.*

CHAPTER
21

NO SPOTS,
NO WRINKLES

I couldn't help but lament to the Lord, "God, I hope our generation doesn't have to die off before racism dies in America." At that moment I was just not sure if the people of this great nation have what it will take to bring about the healing needed for this big ugly sore to heal over and finally go away. Attempting to process the racial tsunami that I did not see coming at the Cru conference in 2015, I recognized how ill-prepared we all were to deal with our country's age-old problem.

Between conference sessions the five thousand plus missionary staff walked around like the blind man whose eyes had been touched by Jesus; we still could not see clearly. And like the blind man in Mark 8:22–25, we may need another touch from Jesus to erase the stain of sin in the area of race and inequality to see things clearly—to see people as people, to see all people equally.

And they came to Bethsaida. And some people brought to him a blind man and begged him to touch him. And he took the blind man by the hand and led him out of the village, and when he had spit on his eyes and laid his hands on him, he asked him, "Do you see anything?" And he looked up and said, "I see people, but they look like trees, walking." Then Jesus laid his hands on his eyes again; and he opened his eyes, his sight was restored, and he saw everything clearly.

(Mark 8:22–25)

My mind was whirling from the various speakers, the content, and Cru's courage to turn to face the elephant in the room. We were forced to look at the gaping wound that has been festering for centuries—the wound that had just been traumatically reinjured by the epic assault on African American Christians attending a noonday Bible study at the Mother Emmanuel AME Church. And while the racial divide has had a scab over it for most of our lives, it is still infected and festering. This reality is evident by the pain I was experiencing and the confusion, sorrow, and denial my fellow missionaries were experiencing. We were in the same stadium hearing the same speakers but having a much different experience.

I'll ask you, my brothers and sisters in Christ, the same question I ask myself: What business do we (the church) have with the sin of pride and prejudices, superiority, injustice, and inequality when Christ has redeemed us with His blood and death on the cross, so that He may present us to Himself? "So that he might present the church to himself in splendor, without spot or wrinkle or any such thing, that she might be holy and without blemish." (Eph. 5:27) Indeed, Jesus is coming back for His church one day—a church that He will present to Himself in splendor.

Is our only hope out of this complex centuries-old quagmire the next generation? Will we be like the children of Israel described by Moses in Deuteronomy 1, when God denied a whole generation of Israelites access to the promised land because of their disobedience? How many times and how many years must we circle this same old mountain?

I am hopeful that our next generation of Christians can put aside racial division and unite as one in Christ. I feel like *the* best thing my generation has done as Americans is raise our children not to judge people by their cultural background or the color of their skin. I'm so encouraged by the attitude of my son's generation toward accepting others. Maybe there is hope for us yet to embrace what we seem to have imparted to our children. I'm optimistic that it's not too late! We have it in us to do the right thing; our children are proof of that. Take notice of your children's friends. Are they not an array of hues and ethnicities? Are they not from various backgrounds and cultures? They are happily united by a common set of values, likes, and interests!

How is it that we can pass down what is right? Instinctively we know what is right, and wanting what is best for our children, we gave them the better option—the right option. By and large we trained and coached them into a more inclusive culture than our generation had. Somehow suppressing prejudices and biases we painted a vision that is more accepting and inclusive of others. As for us Christians, I stand on the hope that is in the apostle Paul's writings to the Galatians: "So in Christ Jesus you are all children of God through faith, for all of you who were baptized into Christ have clothed yourselves with Christ. There is neither Jew nor

Gentile, neither slave nor free, nor is there male and female, for you are all one in Christ Jesus" (Gal. 3:26–28, NIV).

As we grapple with our individual storylines, I think the bigger questions is, how is being one in unity with our brother and sisters in Christ actually lived out in each of our lives? Let us recognize the wrong in our thinking, acts, and deeds. Let's refrain from the faulty rush to judgment and the problematic biases that are never true of entire peoples and ethnicities. Thankfully, God gives us a blotter to blot out parts of our story with confession and repentance. The parts of our story that we don't like and would like to get a do over, we have but to confess our sins, as the apostle John says, "If we confess our sins, he is faithful and just to forgive us our sins and to cleanse us from all unrighteousness" (1 John 1:9).

When we confess our sins to God, it is equivalent to taking a black Sharpie and blotting out excerpts of our story that we are not proud of, or like taking Magic Eraser and wiping out our wrongdoings. And when we do this, God is faithful to forgive us of our sins. Let us cry out to the Lord as King David did in Psalm 25:7: "Do not remember the sins of my youth, nor my transgressions; according to Your mercy remember me, for Your goodness' sake, O LORD" (NKJV). Or when David begs the Lord, "Have mercy upon me, O God, according to Your lovingkindness; according to the multitude of Your tender mercies, blot out my transgressions" (Ps. 51:1, NKJV).

God's character and approach to our sin are expressed in the book of Isaiah, "I, even I, am He who blots out your transgressions for My own sake; and I will not remember your sins" (Isa. 43:25, NKJV).

Dear Lord,

Your Word tells us to confess our sins to one another and pray for one another so that we may be healed, because the prayer of a righteous person has great power as it is working. Father God, I confess that I have biases and prejudices that I am ashamed of. Help me to see people as You see them.

Lord Jesus, I acknowledge my sin to You, and I no longer hide my guilt. I confess my wrongdoings to You, Lord. You alone forgive the guilt of my sin. Lord, as I turn to You in repentance, thank You for blotting out my sins. I am forever grateful!

In the day of Your return, Lord Jesus, I pray that we the church may be that splendid church, without spot or wrinkle. May we be presentable to You, holy, and without blemish. In the name of Jesus, I pray. Amen. (James 5:16; Psalms 32:5; Acts 3:19; Ephesians 5:27)

FIRST FIX US

"Lord, our country is broken. And the church is broken. And Lord, we are broken at Cru too! But if we can fix Cru, we can then roll it (being one in Christ) out to the church, and then maybe we can affect our country," I lamented before the Lord as I considered yet another assignment I dreaded.

Exactly one month after my mother passed away in the fall of 2019, I received a call from a friend of mine at Cru, excited to tell me about a position for which he thought I would be perfect. He followed his call up with this email connecting me to the chief of staff for Oneness and Diversity at Cru.

Hi there Pam!

I wanted to take this opportunity to introduce you to a very dear colleague of mine here at Lake Hart. Chris Pratt and I worked together in the USDEV office over the past 4 years. Last summer he transitioned to the Office of Oneness and Diversity (I think I got that name right). He also currently has management responsibilities with the SLI program.

I have been telling Chris everything I know about you, Pam. I'm most impressed that besides being an experienced development officer you are humble, eager to learn new things and super smart. You have a deep love for Cru/StoryRunners and can see clearly how God has put the pieces of your life together for this time. You are poised, gracious in speech and warmly communicate to others how much you care and value them.

Anyway, I would love for you two to connect either by video call or here in Orlando next time you come by. (I can't help myself—I love connecting people together especially people I really like and respect!)

The description of the director of communications role read *develops and executes communication strategies for Oneness and Diversity, utilizing various media platforms to effectively represent the O&D message priorities to all audiences.* I cringed at the thought of getting in the middle of any discussion, written or verbal, about diversity. The thought horrified me. I've seen what happens to people on social media who voice their opinion one way or another about race, unity, or diversity, and I wanted no part of it. But I couldn't ignore the tug at my heart, which I knew was God's calling me into this role. I began to sob and beg God to find someone else, all the while knowing He had been preparing me for this. "But I just want to live a quiet, unassuming life of service to You, Lord." My pleas continued to no avail.

Over the next couple of weeks, the Lord showed me that this position would allow me to have safe and loving conversations with my Christian sisters and brothers about the division we experience as His children and how He desires for us to love one another and be one in Him, just as He prayed to the Father in John 17. I felt the heart ties begin to form in my spirit, and the thought of oneness in Christ Jesus was something I began to want for my Christian family and myself. The mystery of being surrendered to God, having said yes to His call on your life, is that you don't know the *all* to which you have said yes. God reveals *all* along the way. Imagine if God told us all that we are agreeing to up front; many of us would not go along so willingly with our enthusiastic, "Yes Lord."

For decades my missional focus has been strictly evangelism driven, winning souls for Christ with emphasis on getting God's Word to unreached people groups and specifically those who do not have Scripture in their language or cannot read the Bible written in their language. But the more I spent time in Scripture experiencing Jesus' love and desire for His followers to be one in complete unity, the bigger my burden grew for Christians from all ethnicities to fully understand and love one another. My heart began to align with Jesus' desire and prayer for all believers to be in Him and the Father so that the world with whom we share will know that God sent Jesus into the world. I began to see that oneness and the unity of believers are tied to the gospel going forth and how it is tied to the completion of the Great Commission. Jesus wants the world to know that God sent Him. I knew in my spirit that this was also an important part of my calling. According to Jesus, our oneness is for the sake of the gospel spreading to the world.

My prayer is not for them alone. I pray also for those who will believe in me through their message, that all of them may be one, Father, just as you are in me and I am in you. May they also be in us so that the world may believe that you have sent me. I have given them the glory that you gave me, that they may be one as we are one—I in them and you in me—so that they may be brought to complete unity. Then the world will know that you sent me and have loved them even as you have loved me.

(John 17:20–23, NIV)

Again and again, fear gripped me, and I would resist and pray until I finally surrendered to a feeling of being enveloped in Jesus' love and an understanding of His heart's desire for His followers to be the answer to His prayer—complete unity. I let His Word continue to wash over me, allowing me to see how believers' unity is a testimony to nonbelievers that God sent Jesus into the world. *Being one wins souls.* Unity is a soul-winning strategy and therefore, being one is a strategic part of Win, Build, Send, which is the Cru DNA and what I said yes to. Being one—complete unity is the attraction that draws the world into discovering that Jesus is the Son of God, sent by God the Father into the world so that the world may believe in Him.

This timeless prayer is also for those who will believe in Him. It's for the *whosoevers* of all generations from all the nations. That includes us as believers because, when Jesus prayed this prayer, we were the future believers for whom He was interceding. Jesus peers down through the corridors of the future (the yet-to-come) and intercedes for you and me. You and I were among those who had not yet believed but will believe. We are an answer to His prayer, since "God so loved the world, that he gave his only Son, that whoever believes in him should not perish but have eternal life" (John 3:16).

Being one is not just for the sake of unity in God's family; it also succeeds in attracting the world to the Father through Jesus Christ. Imagine our unity being so winsome to the world that people from every nation, tribe, and tongue, both here in our country and abroad, would want to be part of God's family. We see a demonstration of this among the early church in Acts 2:46–47. There is no they, them, or those people. On the contrary, verse 44 says, "All the believers were together and had everything in common" (NIV). In John 17:22, Jesus tells the Father that He has even given us His glory, the same glory the Father gave Him so that we could be one like the two of them are one. Sisters and brothers in Christ, our testimony of being one in Christ propels the gospel forward. By giving us His glory, Jesus gave us the power to be one. Furthermore, if we are committed to spreading the gospel to the whole world, it stands to reason that we would become one so that the world may believe that God sent Jesus and the Great Commission be completed. We can be the answer to His prayer. Don't you want to be the answer to Jesus' prayer? Let's be the answer to Jesus' prayer.

We see Paul making this same plea to the church at Ephesus, when he implores them, "Make every effort to keep the unity of the Spirit through the bond of peace" (Eph. 4:3, NIV). When we join the family of God by putting our faith in Jesus Christ, we are positioned or placed in Christ and become part of the body of Christ.

169

> *There is one body and one Spirit, just as you were called to one hope when you were called; one Lord, one faith, one baptism; one God and Father of all, who is over all and through all and in all.*
>
> *(Eph. 4:4–6, NIV)*

If being one were lived out and embraced as an intentional mission strategy on our part, how many more could we win? How many more would believe if seekers saw God's children getting along like the family for whom Jesus gave His life? He gave His life to bring us into a right relationship with God and into the family of God. And like any blended family, we may have skirmishes over turf in the beginning, but eventually, we learn to get along for the sake of the parents who love each other and want to see us get along and be a family.

That is what Jesus is asking the Father for after He commands us to love one another just two chapters earlier in John 15:17.

Dear Lord,

I pray that our love for one another would be so powerful and glorious that people everywhere who witness this great love would flock to You and want to know Jesus as their Lord and Savior. Lord, please help us put aside the differences that divide us and draw on what makes us alike. We all call You our heavenly Father and are all redeemed by the blood of Your Son and adopted into Your family. And we are all in Christ Jesus.

Lord, we look to You and plead with You to make us one not just in name only (the church) but at the heart level. Give us an overwhelming desire to be a united family—Your one big happy family. Please work in our hearts and remove all that divides us, oh Lord. Please make us one, just as Jesus prayed. I pray this prayer in the name of Jesus, Your beloved Son, who gave His life for us to be Your children. Amen!

CHAPTER
23

BE SPLENDID

By now, you may be asking yourself, what's next? What do I do now with this new awareness and sensitivity to how people, especially my sisters and brothers in Christ, experience life? I have poured my heart out and shared some of my personal story and hopefully most insightful experiences. I have searched my past and my soul to share what I think are the most helpful parts of my life regarding this assignment God gave me. I can't tell you with certainty what will happen next. What I can only tell you is what I hope will happen.

I hope all of God's children will make room in our hearts and actual spaces for all people regardless of color. I hope the days I walk into a room of leaders to discover that I am the only Black person there are a thing of the past. I hope achieving another title of "the first Black" is not a repeat occurrence, because that would signify the doors of opportunity and inclusion have not been welcoming to people who look like me. I hope neither I nor anyone who looks like me feels isolated, alone, or intimidated by the scarcity of diversity in a given space.

I know that to improve the outlook and trajectory of our society will take effort, persistence, and lots of courage on the part of Christians. And yes, this country's citizenry must also desire a united, harmonious future together, which we have heard about from visionaries of our past in terms like "a more perfect union" as countrymen. But for now, I believe followers of Jesus are the best hope for our country's unity. I am hopeful that Christians will unite as one in Christ, not only in position but in Christlike love, lived out for the world to see. "Having purified your souls by your obedience to the truth for a sincere brotherly love, love one another earnestly from a pure heart" (1 Peter 1:22). Or as Jesus said, "A new commandment I give to you, that you love one another: just as I have loved you, you also are to love one another. By this all people will know that you are my disciples, if you have love for one another" (John 13:34–35).

Be honest, believers, would the world know that God sent Jesus and He loves them by our testimony lived out before them? Does our testimony glorify God? If you can say, "Yes, my testimony is an example of being one and in complete unity with other believers," then carry on in your walk so that the world will come to know God's love for them. But if you are saying "I don't feel like my example of unity is one to be followed," thank you for your honesty. Please take some time to reflect on the adjustment you will make to be brought to complete unity with your brothers and sisters in Christ.

In God's Word, the beloved church is called His bride (Rev. 19:7) and His body (1 Cor. 12:27). As people of God—the church—we have a higher, holier directive to be one, united in Christ Jesus. We, the church—a body of believers—are *the group of people* genuinely motivated to be one, united in our Lord and Savior Jesus Christ. We are the only people who have *a prayer* of being unified as people of God, who live as the body and bride of Christ. The world does not know the Father and, therefore, is not motivated or inspired to behave as one united people. But we are united by Christ, having received the same Word, and have been given His glory that we may be one, sanctified in truth and sent into the world (John 17).

When you envision our country's future, do you see the people's harmonious existence, or do you see discord and mayhem? The profoundness of this moment is that we get to decide how we will show up. We, Christian Americans occupying this time in history, get to determine how our book of Acts will read and affect our country—our future and the future of our children and grandchildren. What we do right now in this precise moment will determine what's next. Christian brothers and sisters, even when the culture around us gets it wrong, let's prevent our country from this free fall that we are in (that seems to be picking up speed), by being distinctly different. Let us deliberately manifest the glory of God that has been given to us. "The glory that you have given me I have given to them, that they may be one even as we are one, I in them and you in me, that they may become perfectly one, so that the world may know that you sent me and loved them even as you loved me" (John 17:22–23).

I hear you saying, "But I don't know what to do." Indeed, behaving as brothers and sisters in Christ and loving one another as the family of God can be the single most powerful witness to our nation and the world. You may be like me and want to sit on the sidelines and stay out of the fray. The idea of being front and center in this discourse is *scary*. I know. Trust me; I get it.

Right now is where courage comes in, because when you think of the alternative, that's even scarier. Here is what we do: grab hands with someone who doesn't look like us and begin creating a genuine friendship, an unbreakable bond. Create a relationship that is understanding and gracious. Let's start there and see where that takes us. Then add another to your circle of friends—then another, creating a diverse circle of Christian friends. We can do this. What we can't do is nothing. "Therefore be imitators of God, as beloved children. And walk in love, as Christ loved us and gave himself up for us, a fragrant offering and sacrifice to God." (Eph. 5:1–2)

We are the salt and the light. If we do nothing and refuse to shine, then darkness encroaches. We must persist in steadfastly shining our light in the world and watching the darkness flee. "You are the salt of the earth…You are the light of the world…Let your light shine before others, so that they may see your good works and give glory to your Father who is in heaven." (Matt. 5:13, 14, 16) I am optimistic that there is more than enough light to illuminate the darkness in our world and in our country. Let us turn our light from dim to illuminate brighter and brighter, forcing back the darkness.

If you are wondering, what can I do? What intentional steps can I take toward unity? Here are some first steps I encourage you to take on this journey:

- Become friends with someone of another ethnicity.

- Visit a church where the majority of members look different from you.

- Invite someone from another ethnicity to your church or home or to coffee.

- Read a book about the struggles of minorities or people from a different ethnicity.

- Read an article or a blog that challenges your current thinking and resist the urge to comment.

- Bring a tray of fresh-baked cookies to your Christian neighbor who looks different from you.

- Start a diverse neighborhood Bible study or book club.

I also encourage you to ask yourself some tough questions:

> What else do I not see or have I not seen?
>
> What else have I missed or do I not know?
>
> What else do I not understand or need to understand?
>
> What have I looked away from or ignored?
>
> What have I grown comfortable not knowing?
>
> Is there anyone God has brought to mind that I can befriend?

It is my sincere hope that by giving you a peek into my life, you will be encouraged to seek knowledge and understanding of different and diverse communities of those in the margins and those in the majority. By opening up and sharing some of my experiences and my heartache, my desire is that my story will cause each of us to examine ourselves with the intention of not staying the same but with the expectation to grow in our desire for complete unity.

I believe it starts with inner work at the heart level. Inner work is a wonderful opportunity to embrace the true reality of our condition, bring it before the Lord, and deal with it privately before our loving God. Only you and God really know how you feel about such matters. This private work allows us to be totally honest with ourselves without others' judgment, without condemnation, without shame or blame. This inner work allows the all-important thought process to happen, identifying the root of the problem, discovering the origin of the problem, the intensity of the situation, and the sincerity of our desire to change and grow.

This inner work is for anyone and everyone who has biases, preferences, or even prejudices—I think that's all of us. In our fallen human condition, it is only natural for this to be the case. But we were bought with a price—the blood of Jesus. And when He bought us and adopted us into the family of God, we became new creatures with a new nature. Now we have the Spirit of the living God living in us to help us be more like Christ. The Spirit of God prompts our conscience and becomes our guide, letting us know through small prompting and dis-ease when our character, actions, and even thoughts do not resemble Christlikeness. And if we listen to the prompting of the Holy Spirit and self-correct, we will find ourselves growing into a Christlikeness that is more and more splendid.

One day, Christ will return for the church, a splendid church to present to Himself. The church is not a building or an edifice or a temple. It is the people who gather in the church house or temple of God. So how do we, the people of God, become that splendid church? We begin with prayer and a desire to be a more splendid church. And because we are individual members of the church, we become splendid ourselves. You may ask yourself, what does a more splendid me look like?

How does a more splendid me improve on the way I think? How does a more splendid me act, and what does my character reveal? This could take some reimagining of ourselves. I love the reimagining process. Just the thought of it brings a huge smile to my face when I think beyond who I am now to who God is re-creating me to be. I get excited about the possibilities.

I will continue to pray that as believers in Christ Jesus we mature in our faith and desire to be more united in Christ. And that we see one another as made in God's image, the *imago Dei*, causing us to renew our minds so that we can go beyond seeing but also treating one another as we are—made new creatures in Christ, redeemed by Christ Jesus, and therefore all in Christ. If we would simply follow what Jesus deemed the greatest commandments in Matthew 22:37–39: "'You shall love the LORD your God with all your heart, with all your soul, and with all your mind.' This is the first and great commandment. And the second is like it: 'You shall love your neighbor as yourself'" (NKJV). The Amplified Bible says that loving our neighbor is to "unselfishly seek the best or higher good for others." Now, I'm not saying we don't love everyone, but to initiate exponential impact, if our emphasis were to love and show love to our Christian neighbors, for starters, we the church could be the change agents our country so desperately needs right now, at this moment in our country's history.

Brothers and sisters, let us truly become united—one in Christ so that the world may know we are followers of Jesus, the one God sent into the world that they may also follow Him. Let us be the answer to Jesus' prayer in John 17 and the fulfillment of His splendid church in Ephesians 5 that Christ gave Himself up for, to present to Himself in splendor.

Let us be united!
Let us be one!
Let us be that splendid church!